Praise for Holli Kenley's *Mountain Air*

"I love *Mountain Air*! I could relate to it so much. *Mountain Air* takes you on a rippling effect of a journey of healing, with the ups and downs of the healing process. You are on a continuous cycle of feeling better, then plagued with a reminder of the past that sets you back. There are periods of time where you regress back into unhealthy behaviors when you lose focus on how to love you for who you are and not for the damage that was done to you in the past/childhood. As a survivor of childhood sexual abuse, I could relate to the message given in *Mountain Air*. I would recommend this book to anyone in recovery."

—Marie Waldrep, author,
A Voice That Has Spoken From Within

"I have read *Mountain Air* twice and have taken the opportunity for personal reflection. Your book has again reaffirmed for me how life teaches the lessons we need wherever we are. In my work as a therapist, I have been privileged to participate in my clients' courageous journeys from pain to healing. At times, they have had to struggle with the frustrating challenges of relapse. With commitment, they have been able to process and incorporate the new lessons learned as they moved from emotional birth, through death, to rebirth. Holli Kenley expresses this flow in a very personal and powerful way. With guided reflections, she offers the readers the opportunity to embrace their pain and move toward healing. She also presents professionals with a tool to augment their clinical work."

—Elizabeth Soeth, M.A., MFT

Holli Kenley's *Mountain Air* is a refreshing look at the process of relapse and recovery. Who better to offer insight than someone who has lived the dark night of the soul and come out the other side. Holli's self-disclosure makes this book so unique. I particularly liked the inclusion of Nature and the seasons as healing tools. As Holli writes, 'Nature taught me long ago that resiliency is a finely blended outgrowth of devastation and courage'. Discussion questions at the end of each chapter make this into a workbook for recovery as well as a healing story. I will recommend it for my clients."

—Carol Teitelbaum, MFT, Rancho Mirage, California
Founder of www.CreativeChangeConferences.com and
It Happens to Boys Project for men abused as children.

"Using the strength and power of nature's lessons, *Mountain Air* provides a message of hope and the strategies to get there. For all who feel they have compromised their time, values, and integrity to the extent they have lost themselves and are now seeking a path back to their truth and authentic self, this is a must read. With Holli's inspiring personal journey from relapse to recovery and her challenging questions in each chapter, the reader can examine self-defeating behaviors and beliefs that block the natural ability to walk through change, pain, and difficult times. A unique and comprehensive approach for both individuals and clinicians to use as a guide for relapse prevention and recovery."

—Melissa Yarbray, M.A., Marriage and Family Therapist,
Licensed Advanced Alcohol & Drug Counselor

"Holli Kenley, psychotherapist and abuse-survivor herself, has created a work that is unique in the recovery literature. Her particular focus is on the inevitable relapses along the way to healing. Recovery is not a straight line ascent but rather a spiral in which the old issues, temptations, and fears come around again, challenging us to meet them at a higher level of functioning. Without going into the history of her abuse, her book is nevertheless a personal memoir out of which she extracts principles that can be generalized to all who are in recovery, inspiring them to take courage. This poetic and nature-infused account should become a standard for all therapists and all in the process of recovery."

—David Van Nuys, Ph.D., Emeritus Professor of Psychology
Host, *Shrink Rap Radio*

"Sustained wellness must be maintained. Holli Kenley takes us on a journey mirrored in the beautiful allegory of nature as she reclaims her true self. Come alongside her as she sheds layers of unhealthy behaviors, thoughts, and feelings... once again finding peace and the ability to breathe in life."

—Julie Hauck, R.N.

"*Mountain Air* is a learning tool. It not only provides journaling prompts which allow the readers to become participants in their healing, but it does so in such a meaningful way. Holli Kenley's ability to share the lessons that she learned from Nature and her own life are inspiring. It makes me want to take more time and 'listen' to the messages that are right in front of me—the ones Nature provides. As Holli masterfully crafts both story and emotion, she writes to help others who are struggling and to help loved ones by providing them with greater insight into the topic of relapse."

—Diana Cinatl, M. A. Education, International Baccalaureate
Coordinator Secondary Education

Mountain Air

Relapsing And Finding the Way Back...
One Breath at a Time

Holli Kenley, M.A., MFT
Foreword by Jondra Pennington

Loving Healing Press

Foreword by Jondra Pennington
Author photos by Julianna Calin
Learn more at www.HolliKenley.com

Library of Congress Cataloging-in-Publication Data

Kenley, Holli, 1951-
Mountain air : relapsing and finding the way back... one breath at a time / Holli
Kenley, M.A., MFT ; introduction by Jondra Pennington.
pages cm -- (New horizons in therapy series)
Includes bibliographical references and index.
ISBN 978-1-61599-188-4 (pbk. : alk. paper) -- ISBN 978-1-61599-189-1
(hardcover : alk. paper) -- ISBN 978-1-61599-190-7 (ebook)
1. Kenley, Holli, 1951- 2. Substance abuse. 3. Recovering addicts--United
States. 4. Nature, Healing power of. 5. Mind and body. I. Title.
HV4998.K46 2013
362.29092--dc23
[B]
                              2012051770

Distributed by Ingram Book Group, Betram's Books, New Leaf

Published by
Loving Healing Press
5145 Pontiac Trail
Ann Arbor, MI 48105

Phone: 888-761-6268
Fax: 734-663-6861

www.LHPress.com
info@LHPress.com

For The Recovering

My truth is mine and mine alone,
It centers me and comforts me.
I share it freely and honestly,
Helping others to honor their own.

Also by Holli Kenley

Pilates For Parenting: Stretch Yourself and Strengthen Your Family

Another Way: A Novel

Power Down & Parent Up!: Cyber Bullying, Screen Dependence & Raising Tech-Healthy Children

Breaking Through Betrayal: And Recovering the Peace Within, 2nd Edition

Daughters Betrayed By Their Mothers: Moving From Brokenness To Wholeness Perfect Bound

Contents

Table of Exercises

Acknowledging our paths

Loving Healing Press, Inc.—
Publisher Victor Volkman, Editor Ernest Dempsey, and Staff
Our paths first crossed in the Winter of 2009,
Thank you for your unwavering belief in my work,
And for your commitment to empowering the healing community.

Lani Stoner—
Fellow Therapist and Trusting Friend
Our paths connected in the Fall of 2008,
Thank you for your extraordinary talents in editing, revising, and clarifying,
And for your continual investment into the wellness of others.

Diana Cinatl—
Longtime Teacher Colleague and Forever Friend
Our paths intersected in the Summer of 1988,
Thank you for your ability to fine-tune a piece of writing,
And for the immeasurable compassion you gift upon others.

Dan Kenley and Alexis Shoemate—
Loving Husband and Precious Daughter:
Our paths have joined and intertwined over a lifetime,
Thank you for loving me through the journeys,
And for the joy of loving you in return.

Foreword

As a psychotherapist, reading books about the human condition is part of the job. We read for a myriad of reasons: to learn how to help the people who come to our offices looking for a way out of their pain; to be enlightened by encountering different ways to think about the world; to be moved and inspired by someone's struggle; as well as their defeat or victory in that struggle. Most of the time, we read with the client in mind; but every so often, we read an account of someone's pain and it resonates deep inside us. Such was the case for me when I picked up *Mountain Air*.

Unaware that this experience of my dear friend and colleague was touching something I hadn't looked at before, I found that I could only read it in small doses, unable to tolerate any more than that before a puzzling visceral gut feeling became nearly intolerable. Then one day, in a moment of stillness, it came to the surface that I had pushed down, shoved away, buried an entire six-month period of time in my life where, like Holli, I made a move that I thought would be the very best thing I could do, but resulted in losing my footing and going into a free-fall of confusion and panic as I felt myself slipping away. Instead of feeling confident and sure of myself and my decisions, my days were filled with anxiety, depression, sleepless nights, fear, loneliness, and questions... lots of questions: "why was this happening?" "how could I have been so wrong?" "is there an end to this pain?" and, if so, "how will I survive until I get there?".

Jumping ahead, it took time, but I did find my way back, and I promptly took the events of the previous six months and pushed them way into the background, covered them up with a big black tarp, and never looked back.... until now.

To a therapist, burying painful events is a big no-no. We encourage and guide people as they pull back the covering on pain and accompany them through the mess it leaves in its wake. I never thought I would need to do that for myself. Arrogance? *No.* Denial? *Most certainly.*

Once I realized that there was unfinished emotional business to take care of, I used the relapse and recovery that is shared in *Mountain Air*, as my guide and companion. This wasn't hard to do, given the tender and validating style in which it is written. I began by giving myself permission to go as slow as I needed to go so I could drink in every element of the story and how it relates to my experience. The questions at the end of the chapters facilitated going deeper into what happened to me emotionally during those six months. They also helped me see in a very personal way that the recovery process really isn't linear. The process ebbs and flows, but with each ebb, there are lessons to hold onto as life inevitably flows forward again.

With *Mountain Air*, Holli has made a major contribution to the world of recovery in all its forms. No doubt this book will find its way into the offices of many psychotherapists, into treatment centers, and onto the recommended reading lists of those in the recovery field. Her contribution to the profession is without question. But, Holli has gone a step further into a place only a handful of therapists go: sharing a deeply personal and painful life experience in such brutal detail. Her willingness to do so shows you, the reader, that you are not alone; there is nothing shameful about relapsing, that recovery is most definitely possible, and that on the other side of that relapse is strength and peace.

I pray that you are as blessed as I was as you use *Mountain Air* as part of your own journey back to wholeness.

—Jondra Pennington, M.S., LMFT

Preface

Don't stay long in the shame-filled grounds of relapse,
Fertile soil awaits your return and your recovering.

I believe that life is about recovering and about rejoicing. Many of us who have experienced pain in its many forms and faces have also had the opportunity to embrace recovering from it. It is an on-going journey—one that requires a steadfast spirit and an uncompromising commitment. It is a path that brings us our greatest feelings of peace and of purpose; it is a road to living life to its fullest and at its truest. At the same time, no degree of recovering or of healing knowledge can guarantee a relapse-free life. Relapse is a very real part of recovering; and thus, it is worthy of our attention.

This book is for anyone who has experienced the hard work of recovering and who has rejoiced in its rewards. It is for anyone who has encountered relapse along the way; however, this book addresses relapse in the broad sense of the word. It is for any individual who has returned to or regressed into a pattern of behavior that is unhealthy or unsafe. It is for those individuals who have abandoned their authentic ways of being for a life of personal neglect, of indulgence, or of self-destruction. The book speaks to the addict who has lost his sobriety, to the abused who has returned to her abuser, or to the codependent who has given up his resources once again to rescue the uncontrollable. This book also reaches out to individuals who have maintained a life of stability and wellness, but who have found themselves eroding over time, disappearing, and losing their sense of self and of spirit. It is for the person who has fallen away from a life that is not congruent with the truths that he/she has chosen to invest into, trust in, or believe in. It is for anyone who has forfeited his way of being and who is fighting to find his way back.

Mountain Air: Relapsing and Finding The Way Back One Breath At A Time is a brutally honest personal narrative covering a three-year period of time, from the summer of 2008 through the summer of 2011. At the beginning of each chapter, I write in the present tense, describing my current circumstances and my decent into relapse. After each chapter's introductory section where I disclose the painful decline of my healthy way of being, I take the reader back in time to a sustained season of wellness in my life's healing journey. In each flashback (which is separated in the text with *italics*), I share with the reader a series of relapse lessons and the recovering messages within each. It is in the recalling of these messages that I am able to reclaim their meanings, reintegrate them into my life, and return to healthier ground. Although there are typically several lessons within each chapter, the following theme words describe the essence of each in relation to relapse: Chapter One—Losing one's self; Chapter Two—Lessons lost; Chapter Three—Relapse is relentless; Chapter Four—Shame; Chapter Five—The restraints of relapse; Chapter Six—Seeds of doubt and disappointment; Chapter Seven—A fearless inventory; Chapter Eight—Releasing; Chapter Nine—Reclaiming one's self and one's truth; Chapter Ten—Home; Epilogue—Rewards.

As I share my relapse journey with you, I invite the reader to take an active part in your healing work as well. At the end of each chapter, there is a series of topics for reflective journaling and recovering exercises embedded within them. Choose a time and place that is safe and free of distractions. Although topics may be difficult to think back upon or about, set a comfortable pace for yourself as you write honestly and openly about your experiences. Acknowledging and expressing your painful injuries, injustices, or inadequacies is the first step in breaking through a period of relapse or an episode of regression into unhealthy life patterns. Secondly, learning how to make healthy choices and then acting upon them will help you to maintain and sustain a well way of being.

Let's begin our recovering—together.

Holli Kenley
Spring 2013

The First Wind—Facing West

"To you, the west, where dreams take wing
and day comes to a rest,
hear me, and keep this image from me."

— Kent Nerburn

One—Mountain Fire

Summer 2008

In July 2008, I chose to return to the environment of my youth. No one encouraged me or coerced me. I did so of my own free will. I felt like a foreigner feigning blending in and yet fighting to insulate myself from the toxins around me. Coming from a mountain habitat, the surrounding landscape shocked my system and strangled my senses. The air was grayish-brown with a hint of blue struggling to break through the giant igloo encapsulating the valley. The smells from the sprawling agricultural fields triggered reminders of planes scattering pesticides and my sinuses burned as I breathed in microscopic pollutants. Just beyond the walls of the manicured development where we purchased our new home were clusters of over-crowded animal farms. The feeding corrals and the piles of manure blended into one mass of fermented fumes. Each time I drove by the nauseous odor, I felt sickened by the inhumanity of it all and questioned its existence.

On a still day, while out walking in my neighborhood, I could hear the traffic noises from the nearby congested interstate with massive trucks hauling goods from farms to be placed onto railroad containers. Nightly, as a nearby army depot came alive, I listened to the crashing sounds of loading cargo onto trains with their tired horns signaling their departure to unknown places. The seasonal pressures and demands from crops of valley life created a frantic static in the air that slowly seemed to crowd out the calm from within.

The intense heat of the July summer days brought back memories from childhood as well as a young woman of escaping to cooler ground and of wanting to be anywhere else other than where I was. Even in the evenings when the vast flatlands seemed to sigh as the delta breezes brought relief to their parched crops, I found myself searching for some form of fresh air, some sort of reprieve from the oppression that was forming around me. By the end of the first week, I lay in bed at night thinking about the mountain environment I left. I missed it; I longed for it. Closing my eyes, I allowed myself to recapture the beauty of living in the mountains, and I began to replay its purpose in my life.

* * *

Leaving the desert floor and climbing up a steep windy unpredictable road, the terrain begins to change. Every so often, cacti and sand are replaced with ocotillo clutching massive boulders and century plants struggling to secure space to sprout and then to blossom. A surprise patch of verbena soothes the eye with clusters of wild flowers sprinkling the rocky floor. Ascending further, the topography rapidly changes its dressing, filling out and filling in the openings both on the ground and in the sky. Wild sagebrush is sandwiched amongst the soaring pines and stunted poplars. Jagged rocks make room for smooth mounds of river rock snuggled amidst the lush green grasses and secret streams. The wind finds its voice as it rustles through the forest tapestry.

Suddenly, the serene beauty is transformed by the cry of a nearby eagle soaring from tree top to tree branch or by the startled sound of a squirrel scampering across the road seeking refuge. Following the twists and turns of the road while navigating even higher, one last image completes the picture of perfection—a sprawling bonanza-like valley. And this is home.

Choosing to live here was no accident; it was indeed purposeful. At first sight of this hidden treasure, magical memories from childhood summers sprang forth of mountain escapades with rowdy cousins, and a longing for the freedoms experienced during those carefree days demanded replication. With the purchase of a lot and with the creative powers of many, a human nest was carefully framed and formed high on a hill overseeing the magnificence before it and yet sharing in it. A family settled in and life began to shape itself around the womb of wonder that nourished it. Connecting with Nature became a continual source of renewal and growth. Long walks alone down a quiet mountain road covered in a rug of pine needles produced opportunities to shed the human cloak of heaviness and to release the inner trappings of turmoil. Gathering fallen pine cones and studying the intricacies of each unique shape provided comfort that even with the broken shapes and crushed thorny leaves, their beauty was not diminished. Witnessing the thunderous storms that washed clean the dry needles from thirsty trees and lifted the aromas from the parched plants refreshed the hope that a way of being can be revived or even made better. And after almost twenty years of embracing the secret gifts of Nature came the confidence of finding, nurturing and becoming a person of authenticity and of truth—my truth.

* * *

As I lay in the dark quiet night reflecting upon the images of mountain life, I couldn't help but question my decision to return to my central valley home.

Why did I choose to abandon all that formed the foundation of a sound mind, body, and spirit?

Why did I move back to an environment that had again proven unworthy of return and of my reinvestment?

Why—after all my work to become the real me—would I risk losing myself?

Why had I come here?

As I often did when I was troubled or confused, I turned to Nature and the lessons She taught me over the years. Whether it was in direct contact with Her or drawing on a memory of Her, the ripe teachings within Nature were always there for the devouring. My mind desperately scoured Nature's harvest and recalled such a message from a dozen summers ago.

* * *

When a forest fire swept through the dry foliage near our mountain home, residents were evacuated as were their horses and other beloved animals.

Because of the fearless firemen who were stationed close by, there was no loss of human or domesticated life. However, the wild life—plant and animal—did not fare as well. For a lengthy stretch of miles and an unknown amount of acreage, there was complete devastation. For months, each day driving by the barren landscape with charred limbs and deformed trunks angled mercilessly into its blackened soil, my heart ached. Questions flooded my mind as to causation and yet no answers surfaced. No one came to rebuild or to replant. The summer passed without rescue; the crusted canvass remained foreign among its living distant relatives. Mother Earth remained still, and She waited. One truth lay dormant—fertile soil awaited Her return and Her re-growth.

* * *

As I thought about how I was losing myself in the inner flames of confusion, I remembered the stillness of the charred landscape. Although Nature did not provide me with the answers as to why I chose to enter my fiery betrayal environs or how they were so easily torching my ways of being, for now

She provided me with the one truth I needed. With Her fertile life lessons and guidance, I would find my way back.

Chapter 1—Topics for Journaling & Recovery Work

1. Think about a period of time in your life or an episode when you chose to abandon the foundations of your healthy way of being. Write about this experience with as much detail and description as possible. Take your time and face your truths. Discuss what you lost of yourself in the process.

2. Thinking back upon your experience, also describe your initial feelings and emotions that accompanied this period of relapse or regression. As you identify them; write about why these feelings are so painful to acknowledge. How do these feelings influence and impact your way of being? How do these feelings play a part in the hold that relapse has on you?

Two—Loving the Land

Fall 2008

Within the first few months of my return to the antagonistic environs of my childhood, I found myself fighting against an old but common behavior—the need to rescue and to take care of others. Although I maintained a steadfast commitment to my professional goals and duties, I consistently gave of myself to family causes and concerns that moved me away from the center of my wellness. I knew what I was doing was not healthy for me; and yet, I slipped easily into the old patterns of wanting others to need me and to appreciate me. And when I felt that my expectations for helping others to achieve healthier ways of being were rejected or that my efforts were perceived as controlling, I fell into the old trap of toxic thinking. I started to believe the classic codependent lies—If I just gave more or did more, I eventually could change others for the better; I would finally be well-regarded for my efforts; I would feel more fulfilled. Instead, an angry and sad self started to emerge that had not visited me for years.

One fall afternoon after an extremely tiring weekend, I took a walk in the cookie-cutter complex in which we lived. As I moved past the clean manicured homes, I found myself barely able to put one foot in front of the other. Fatigue clobbered my mind and my body like a heavy wind pushing against trees causing them to bend and to topple. Because of celebratory events over the past couple of days, I committed myself far beyond the parameters of balance and self-care that I was so accustomed to. As I continued to walk, disappointment and exhaustion crippled my stamina. Not far from a man-made lake that was nestled in the core of our housing development, I sat down on a large smooth rock tucked in between a few long green tule and a small stream. As I looked into the clear rippling waters, I saw my reflection, and yet, I didn't see myself. I had forfeited a long standing practice of wellness for a false sense of needing to be needed, and I had already lost of piece of me. I bent down and swept my hand through the cold stream; I touched my face with the drops still left in my palm. As I felt their coolness drip gently down my warm skin, I closed my eyes and imagined the brisk breezes that cleansed the mountain air at this time of the year. My thoughts drifted back to the first valuable lesson that Nature taught me and how that lesson had transformed entirely my way of being. I grieved its loss and craved its return.

* * *

There are sacrifices that come with living full-time in the mountains. "It isn't for everyone," as was often commented by so many of our acquaintances over the years.

"Why do you live so far away from the desert and from work?"

"Why would you drive up that dangerous mountain road every day, twice a day?"

"Why would you live so many miles from everyone and everything? I would never do that."

It was useless to respond to such unknowing comments. The only convincing that could be done was to invite these foreigners to our place of peace and to let them experience it themselves. But for our family, it was never about the dangers that accompanied the extended windy driveway, or the early morning departures and late evening arrivals back home, or the lifestyle adjustments or hardships that were necessary to live in the pines. Our decision to live in Nature's picturesque ponderosa was rooted in love; thus, our ensuing investment into the land grew from that inner abundant resource.

Over the years, I came to appreciate the tremendous amount of work it took to maintain the integrity of our property while protecting the mountain dwelling that had been imposed upon its presence. It was a fine balance of respecting the living gifts that framed and formed the landscape surrounding our man-made structure which we intentionally blended into Nature's canvas of colors and textures. Although our home was perched upon a substantial hillside, a steep stocky hilltop rose up behind the house where it touched cheek to cheek with a bountiful national forest. Fire danger demanded that an invisible line be drawn between manufactured life and true life; thus, a checkerboard sparseness was carefully and delicately created for protection. For almost two dozen years, my husband planted, transplanted, and nurtured a blend of cacti and sage which served plural roles of preventing soil erosion, of replenishing the balding landscape, and of securing a sense of safety in our hearts. This balancing act was replicated within a designated circumference of our beloved dwelling, season after season, and year after year. Although there were times when I found it extremely difficult to cut away or to remove a living piece of our plant family, I trusted that the pruning would make way for new growth or make it safer for the growth that bordered the cleared space.

Loving our land also meant keeping in compliance with the mountain homeowners association's rigid requirements. One such rule was that all fences which bordered the street were to be painted white and kept in proper repair. On purchasing our property, we inherited a weathered wooden fence that needed a severe scraping followed by a fresh coat of paint and over time, it called for numerous reinforcements. Over the first dozen years or so, we managed to mother our orphaned fence until it could no longer hold another coat of paint or withstand another limb replacement. After an inner battle between guarding the authenticity of Nature's wooden design and giving way to the calls of practicality and cosmetic beauty, we succumbed to the adoption of a shiny white vinyl fence. I remember how I felt that Nature had been betrayed by this alien among its midst, and I recall how it took time to see how it served its purpose well by maintaining its strength for years to come. I remember driving up our driveway years later, thinking how its bright beauty actually enhanced the entrance to our home and set a tone of completeness.

While Nature, for the most part, took care of Herself, I felt Her presence on other aspects of my relationship with Her. Whether it was the various little varmints that snuck into our attic, or the thunderous storms slapping against the siding of our home while chipping away its paint and bending its flat surface, or the wood peckers awakening us as they pecked mercilessly at our sterile metal gutters, I welcomed the opportunities to embrace what She taught me and to improve upon lessons learned from Her. With every investment in my life on the hill came the appreciation and the knowing that what I was creating was a new way of being and a new truth—my truth.

I arrived in the mountains not fully aware of how damaged I was. What I did know is that my journey had not been an easy one. Plagued with feelings of insecurity, worthlessness, and inadequacy for most of my life, I had become accustomed to overachieving, trying to fill the voids within. Although successful in academics as well as in the performing arts, shyness masked a spirit screaming for a voice. Maturing into a young woman, I also lived with a restlessness that drove me from relationship to relationship and from place to place. A pattern of running away and escaping reminders of painful childhood memories slowed my racing mind and calmed my anxious heart for short periods of time. And then, I was off again searching for and not finding a refuge for rest and renewal. Wherever I went, the well of worthlessness awaited me, pulling me in and pushing me under. It wasn't until my early thirties that a career opportunity in another part of California presented itself to my loving husband, and along with the job change was my hope that this move might finally bring me a sustained reprieve from the inner turmoil. All the pieces of relocation fell into place at a rapid pace. My precious young daughter, my supportive husband, and I drove away from the valley flatlands and headed into the mountain peaks of Southern California.

After years of floundering, I finally found myself safe in a place of peace, and I began to strengthen my inner core. The serenity, the stillness, and the silence of the mountains wove their way into the fabric of my being. Long quiet walks interrupted with the accompaniment of rustling leaves, the scampering of squirrels up dry pine bark, or of pine cones dropping to their final resting places soothed an inner scab concealing a festering wound. Splashing sparkling creeks gliding over river rocks drew out a portion of the chaos within as I closed my eyes and imagined them carrying tumors of anxiety with them downstream. As I walked briskly and breathed in the pure mountain air, there were days where the strong winds pushed against my will or the snow-covered trails surprised me with slippery steps and funny falls. Still, I walked. I loved the sound of my feet crunching the rain-soaked forest carpets or the tapping of rubber soles on the crystal-clear paths. In these magically serene moments, I raised my head and tilted my face toward Father Sun. The rays touched my skin and thawed a frigid soul. Healing began by being in Nature and by embracing what She had to offer me.

With time, loving the land as I did and reaping the rewards of this love gave me the courage to begin loving myself. Just as I faced the hard work of investing into our mountain dwelling, I began to work through the enormous task of learning to care for myself. This started with the realization that as with the land, in order for new growth to take root and flourish, there was a need for diligent yet thorough removal of overgrown pain-filled foliage.

Just as we meticulously cleared the spaces around our home for protection from fire, I began to clean out the foundations in my life that were not serving me well. Much of the work came in removing the destructive life messages that I internalized from childhood. Unearthing these was like dismembering the roots that feed a fragile plant; although necessary to my re-growth, their removal simultaneously felt like my strangulation. Their toxic fumes had fueled my being for so many years. Slowly, I would unearth one, "I am not good enough." And then another, "I am nothing. I wish I were someone else, anyone else." And then one more, "I don't deserve anything or anyone." And the final one, "I am ugly. I am damaged." As I dug deeply to remove as many debilitating messages as I was aware of and open to at the time, I worked equally as hard to replace them with loving, nurturing seedlings of self-acceptance accompanied with plenty of space for growth and secure boundaries for their protection.

As the years passed, there came a time when the freshly coated messages that I was integrating into my being seemed to be camouflaging an inner brokenness. As with our worn-out wooden fence that required removal of and replacement from its rotting base, I too needed to extricate the pillar of pain lodged deeply in my soul. And just as we had hired an expert to do the painstaking work of digging out the old posts from their cemented foundations, I realized that I could not do my work alone; I needed help. With guidance from a skilled motherly figure, the inner fissure filled with deeply seated fragments of abuse was carefully opened and tenderly cleansed. Exposed to the protective elements guarding and guiding its every transformation, the cauterized wound slowly healed, bringing with it the unveiling of a solid, white shiny structure—a newborn spirit. The hard work continued, and with the passage of time, a more complete being emerged from the rubble supported by an inner core of strength and beauty.

As the infant spirit continued to evolve, I discovered that protection from the toxins of family of origin members and memories of them became paramount to that infant spirit's overall wellbeing and continued growth. However, because of duty or circumstance, there were times where I stepped out of my trusted sources of safety. The carefully crafted spaces we kept clear and distinctly distanced around our mountain home were again reminders of my journey of self-care. Years were spent testing and trying out the safest frequency of my return to the environment that had betrayed me. Visits were methodically spaced and length of stays monitored. Inner borders of safety were implemented. The continual arresting of painful flashbacks along with the constant rehearsal of and replacement with nurturing messages brought fresh water to fragile roots. Recalling the healing paths already journeyed, renaming the lessons learned, and returning to the place of peace within my solid white post allowed me to move through the human wildfire with a retardant of courage and with a shield of confidence.

* * *

Feeling a cool breeze caress my face, my mind struggled to hold onto the images of the recent past. I visualized how my being had been transformed by years of investment and tender care, not only into the land but investing in myself as well. Each one enhanced the other; the elements of Nature blended uniquely with the characteristics of my persona which formed fragrances of new truths. Standing the tests of time, these truths developed their healing potential, filled my soul with loving aromas, and spilled over into other arenas of my life. After countless seasons of emptiness, I had indeed felt full.

As the sun was setting and the temperature was dropping, my concentration lessened its grip on this timeless teaching of Nature. With the gently rippling sounds of the stream bringing me back to my current reality, I opened my eyes. Fixated on my wavy reflection in the splashing waters, once again I was disturbed by its unfamiliarity. I was angry and I was sad. I stood up, but before I walked away, I turned to take one last look into the darkened waters. Watching my reflection dissipate, my eyes were flooded with salty tears. Loving the land had taught me to love myself, but that self-love was vanishing quickly.

Chapter 2—*Topics for Journaling & Recovery Work*

1. Although we do not acknowledge it at the time, when we enter into a period of relapse or regression into unhealthy behaviors, we essentially stop taking care of ourselves. We no longer put our wellbeing first. What are some of the steps, lessons, or measures that you have taken in the past that demonstrate that you "love yourself". List them and discuss their meaning and purpose to your recovering process.

2. After you have identified your protective healing practices of your recovering journey, write about which one/s were lost or let go of easily. Describe how and why they were abandoned. Which one/s were held on to more readily or were retained? Again, describe how and why they were more integrated into your self-care process.

Three—Seasonal Messengers

Winter 2009

One cold winter morning, as I sat at the kitchen table completing research for an article, I looked out the large windows that opened up to the front landscape of our home. Although it was daytime, there was no sunlight coming through the heavy, thick fog that enveloped all living and non-living matter within its grasp. Moving toward the icy glass pane and peering out our plantation shutters to search for some form of life within the ghost-like atmosphere, I found the depth of the fluid grey shield prevented any such discovery. No matter how hard I strained, Nature's images were hidden from me. Although I could not see the leafless trees and brownish-green blades of grass right before me, I knew they were there.

As I returned to the table and my books, I thought about the past few months. The peaceful mindset I arrived with six months previously was difficult to recapture. I knew it was there but as much as I focused and pressed myself to reinstate it, it was slowly disappearing into the fog of self-blame. As often happens when poor choices are made, a pattern of self-recrimination readily engulfs an already depleted state of being. The responsibility I felt for choosing to move back to my betrayal environment and the ensuing erosion of truths wove a shroud of disappointment around me. The heaviness of it all angered me, and I struggled with its ever-tightening grip.

I reminded myself that at this stage of relapse or regression into old behaviors, I needed to step back in order to gain some perspective on the process of recovering. Taking in a few deep breaths, I sat back in my chair, closed my eyes, and relaxed. Allowing my mind to wander into the field of familiar mountain memories, I searched through Nature's lessons I had learned that guided me to an understanding of where I was now and why. Nature proved faithful; Her messengers came forth freely and fully.

* * *

Over the years, the announcement of a seasonal change had more to do with the arrival or departure of characteristic critters than it did Nature's own voice. There were the typical visuals of birds flying in unison heading to southern territories, or the bees swarming around the tops of promising buds, or the sneaky slithering of a rattler looking for an unsuspecting rodent or two. Marking the arrival of spring and making a grand but elegant entrance, a battalion of monarch butterflies descended upon the bottle brush lilac blossoms, which bordered our house. And, there was no ignoring the pesky rabbits feasting on plants that had suffered through a long cold winter only to have their limbs devoured prematurely. Each animal's journey told a story of survival; each animal's behavior signified a choice amidst adversity.

In the late fall and even into winter, it was quite common for deer to saunter close to the rear decking of our home. With a limited assortment of greens at her disposal, a doe would often lead her fawn into the sparse garden. Not far from them, a strong buck kept his eyes on his family and for any elements of danger. Compelled by the forces of hunger, the deer's instincts guided their paths and their inherent survival tools provided them with proven protective measures. Observing the graceful movements of the deer blended with their deliberate awareness, I began to appreciate how delicate their balance was between striving to remain safe among the wild and venturing out toward the human enemy. Trusting in their senses and in the safety of the environment, the deer often wandered right next to our home.

One sunny winter day, I remained at home, nursing a cold and an achy body back to health. Snuggled underneath the brightly colored comforter on my bed, I lay watching the snow melt on the cone-shaped hill behind our house. I marveled at how the white patches clustered around the plants, providing extra moisture to last through the spring months. My eyes dropped down and were drawn to the sterile brick retaining wall that was necessary to hold back erosion during heavy rains and to guide excess runoff down the nearby gorge. My husband had thoughtfully and methodically planted numerous hardy plants to obscure the wall and to blend it into the rock-like formations of the landscape. Turning slightly in bed and resting my head on the coolness of the soft pillow-case, I glanced out another window that opened to the massive meadow below. As I lay still, a poised doe surveyed the area and then she cautiously approached the house. She glided along cautiously; each movement like a careful placement of a dance step. I remained still. She moved in closer, eyeing the plants hiding the retaining wall while nibbling on the foliage by the window. As she chewed, she lifted her head; and in an extraordinary moment, our eyes met. We stared at one another and she moved her face closer. Her nose touched the pane producing a tiny film on it. Our eyes still held one another locked in a timeless truth—with trust comes risk. After a few moments, she lowered her head and devoured more of what she needed. Each bite brought her face back to mine, observing my every movement. Slowly, I shifted my position but the doe remained content. Our connection continued for some time; then with the draw of more enticing food nearby, she paused and faced me one more time—a steady stare filled with knowing and with intention—differentiating between safety and danger. As she gracefully waltzed up the hill, she paused to eat and turned toward me. I sank into the covers and soaked in the silence and stillness of her trusting presence.

In addition to the delicate but deliberate lesson from the deer, other seasonal critters proved valuable in their messages as well. When early mornings were marked by the scamper-like marching of quail traversing the backyard hill, we knew that spring was upon us. Enticing the growing number of quail was birdseed we had purposely chosen for their consumption and had dispersed plentifully. As the weeks passed and their little bodies fattened, it was

remarkable to witness their familiarity with the surrounding gifts of satisfaction as well as their observance for looming dangers. Larger wild animals which inhabited the environs posed a threat upon their survival and the quail would sometimes disappear for days before returning to their eating grounds.

However, with the promise of food, their arrival was guaranteed and their mission unhindered. During one spring season, an unexpected storm dropped over a foot of snow. Frustrated by the burial of their food source, the quail proceeded to perform a protest march around our home. Waddling and sliding across the slippery white ground, the quail attempted to stay in formation. While traversing the snow-covered steep driveway, the quail unknowingly plunged into sunken prints left by human boots. Armed with hungry bellies and with willing wings, the entrapment of each was short-lived. Bursting out of the inverted igloo, every captured quail displayed its remarkable resilience. Relying upon its instincts, retrieving its innate skills, and replicating the movements of its Mother force, each quail forged on without fear. While observing them, I remember thinking that there comes a time when we are so secure in our patterns of behavior and in our thinking processes that they truly become second nature to us. As time passed, I fully acclimated to an environment that served as my source of continual nourishment. And just as the quail demonstrated when faced with adversity, I too navigated from an unwavering source of strength, of confidence, and of resiliency.

Although there were many seasonal messengers who modeled qualities of strong character and formidable spirit, our beloved fox taught me one of my most valuable lessons. It was not unusual for our animal visitors to include coyotes; however, over time a fox or two would often venture onto the property. Although cautious, we would often throw meat scraps out onto the upper part of the hill behind the house. Typically, one or two fox would pick up the tidbits and then dash away toward thicker foliage. One summer, a very small light brown fox with a silver tail started frequenting our hillside buffet. As time passed, he remained while the others departed. My husband started whistling as a signal that "dinner was served."

Quickly, the fox learned the friendly sound and arrived promptly for dinner. As the weeks passed, the little fox became more and more familiar with our routine, and thus became more and more trusting of us. By the end of the summer, the furry friend came right up to the retaining wall where he would take his dinner right from my husband's hand. As the seasons changed, our faithful friend held steadfast. Growing slightly in size, he stayed with us throughout the year, always arriving at the sound of a high-pitched airy call. Each time he crept cautiously and carefully toward us, always grabbed the goodies hastily, and then abruptly stepped back to enjoy his meal. Before departing, he looked to see if there was more; then if not, disappeared into the thicket.

There were times when I wondered how he might survive if we were no longer there to leave his food. I had to remind myself that although the little fox was reliant upon us, instinctively he would know what to do and where to go. The following summer, we left for an extended summer vacation. I knew that upon returning home, our little brown fox would most likely be gone. And, indeed he was. Although there was a sense of guilt for perhaps harming the little guy in some way, there was also a deep sadness. He had become part of my way of being. I witnessed how he learned to trust us, little by little, but still remained rightfully cautious. I saw how he adapted to our feeding rituals but respected and guarded his space as well. Most importantly, the silver and brown furry creature reminded me that when circumstances shift, we must each either embrace the change ahead, or cease to grow and flourish. Choosing to rest upon that truth, I trusted that his time with us served him well. I trusted that our beloved fox, full in his seasonal experience, ventured out to risk survival in territory which had become foreign to him but with time, it too would become familiar.

The more I thought about the messages our seasonal friends had taught me, I began to ponder the idea of choice and of change. Over twenty plus years, I had become accustomed to a diet of Nature which nourished me to fullness and completeness. Investing into my self-care added layers of confidence built on consistency, trust formed from bonds of loyalty, and strength empowered by familiarity. Past insecurities subsided and made room for ample purpose and promise. For the first time in almost two dozen years, I began to ask the question, "Am I ready to leave the mountain?" I turned to Nature and waited for Her guidance. I thought of the silver-tailed fox and of the lessons learned. Secure in my growth and healing, I remained cautious but not fearful. The healing rituals I embraced were well integrated into my way of being and my internal and external spaces were carefully guarded and respected. I recalled all the risks the little fox took, as well as all our other animal friends, and I wondered if I was ready to risk adversity or to confront danger. I again visualized the quail flying out of the snow holes energized and eager to continue their journey. I closed my eyes and replayed the doe's graceful stare of courage and stance of confidence. Again, I asked, "Am I ready to leave the mountain?" I leaned into Nature and waited. All was still. I thought of the brave little fox out in the wild, risking a journey of discovery or possibly one of destruction. It was time I was willing to do the same.

* * *

Allowing Nature's lessons to reside quietly within my being, I leaned forward in my chair and slowly took in a long breath. As it filled my chest and relaxed my body, I experienced a momentary reprieve from the suffocation of self-blame. Recalling my healing journey and recounting the steady movement of growth within the process reminded me that we make choices based on our current levels of recovering. However, we take risks when we choose to do so; relapse is real. As the doe taught me, in choosing our paths, it is always a fine balance of differentiating between what is safe or dangerous. There are no guarantees. As the noose of negative thinking continued to loosen its grip on me, I was humbled by the poignant teachings of all the seasonal messengers.

No matter how resilient the quail or how secure the fox were in their patterns, habits, and instincts to survive in the wild, danger was always present. I was reminded that in recovering there is no room for complacency, or for over-reliance on one's current levels of trust and growth. Most importantly, there is never room for overconfidence in oneself. Outside forces do not rest; neither must the workings of recovering. Pondering these truths, my muscles tightened throughout my body, and my lungs longed for more air. As I glanced out the kitchen window, the wall of fog shifted backwards, lifted just slightly, and then rolled back in like a wave pounding the shore. My eyes watered and burned as I felt the fog of self-blame linger back in, meandering through my mind and swallowing up my spirit.

Chapter 3—Topics for Journaling & Recovery Work

1. In this chapter, we were reminded that relapse is real. Navigating past it requires that we constantly choose between what is safe for us and what is dangerous territory. However, relapse is also relentless; we are incessantly bombarded by its presence. What unhealthy messages, "stinkin' thinkin'", or negative tapes enter your mind that test or influence your decision-making processes? Name them, explain them, and describe their impact on you.

2. Sometimes, our decision-making is weakened by an over-reliance on one's current levels of healing, overconfidence in self, or complacency. Describe how one or all of these have influenced your choices or have contributed to relapse or a return to unhealthy behaviors.

3. Feelings of self-blame and self-pity often emerge during the initial stages of relapse. Describe how these emotions, or others, have affected you and contributed to your relapse and your overall state of being.

Four—Living Trees

Summer 2009

After the first frigid winter and cool spring passed, summer's warmth was a welcome reprieve. As I walked each morning or afternoon, the sun's rays rested on my skin while my bones soaked in their nourishment. The internal thawing of a frozen spirit brought about the re-visitation of an unwanted but not an unexpected feeling—shame. Moving briskly along the walking path of my neighborhood, I felt its ever-present cloak around me. As much as I tried to shake it off, it clung tightly to me.

One afternoon, following a long walk, I returned to our back patio where I enjoyed sitting and listening to the sounds of water falling from a small southwestern fountain strategically placed amidst an array of potted greenery. Resting in the partial shadows provided by the trellised awning and relaxing in the calmness of the moment, I thought about the complexities of the past year and about how incongruent life had become. Part of my life was filled with professional successes and accomplishments. I was achieving goals in my writing and speaking; and most importantly, I was helping others through those venues. I felt strong and confident; I felt well-regarded and well-respected in my field of work. The other part of my life—my personal being—was continuing to spiral down in the wake of relapse. It was embarrassing, frustrating, and painful. Mostly, it was shame-filled.

As I stared at the fountain and watched the water falling from the smallest angled pot dripping down to the next larger one, and then the next until it landed in the bottom one, where it drained into a concealed bowl, I thought about the insidiousness of relapse. Once one enters into the downward spiral of its path, it is almost impossible to climb out of it. It carries us down and as much as we try to surface and to pull ourselves out of it, the weight of shame keeps us tumbling and falling. We search for quick fixes, or grasp for life-lines that will keep us afloat, or seek out diversions that will assuage the pain, but relapse is relentless. For most of us, it isn't until we hit the bottom or until the shame-filled waters spill into the inevitable drain that we have a chance of resurfacing and of recycling back to our fountain of recovering.

As I continued to listen to the gentle splashing sounds and as I thought about how I was struggling against the current of relapse, I recalled Nature's lifelines that I grabbed hold of in my downward spiral. I acknowledged how She had been faithful in guiding and in protecting me with the lessons imparted. However, the more out of control or anxious I felt, the more ineffective I became at implementing them properly. Certainly, they temporarily eased the discomfort of the moment, but the relief was not sustainable. Grasping for some sort of rationale to ease the pain of regression, I began mentally recalling Nature's teachings of many years ago. As my mind wandered back in time, I became frightened. I realized I had neglected one of Her most important lessons.

* * *

Living in the mountains meant cultivating new traditions into our yearly routines and celebrations. Many of them served a dual role: providing pleasure for our family as well as serving a distinct purpose. Along with the implementation of these seasonal practices came the opportunity to meet a host of characters whose lives were uniquely shaped and sculpted by the mountain environment. Although there were many traditions that embellished our way of life on the mountain, there was none more anticipated than that of selecting and securing our annual living Christmas Tree.

In early December, our family started thinking about the characteristics of the new addition that would join our family of living trees already planted and growing. How tall should it be? How full and what kind of pine would complement its surrounding relatives? By the second week of the month and with a flurry of images in each our minds, my husband, daughter, and I excitedly made the short drive to the mountain's best supply of fresh living trees—Harmony Farms. Over the years, we had made friends with the extraverted owner, Larry, and his serene and subdued wife, Joanne. Larry's face glowed with enthusiasm as his friends faithfully arrived each year. With his wiry glasses nestled amidst his fully-bearded face and wild mop of sandy thick hair, Larry's professor-like quality suited him well as he painstakingly cared for each tree according to its particular needs. While bustling around his tree farm greeting his customers and pointing out his favorites, his wife tended to her quaint boutique shop that was filled with custom-made wreaths, homemade jellies, and an assortment of hand-crafted Christmas gifts and goodies. We sauntered around the crowded isles of trees studying each until we discovered just the right one. While my daughter and I paid for the tree and any additional treats we found irresistible, my husband assisted Larry and his eldest son as they moved the heavy tree-filled planter to the front of the farm for delivery later in the day to our home.

As we anxiously awaited the arrival of our newest family member, we prepared its temporary housing inside the great room of our home. With vaulted pine ceilings and expansive windows framing the front of the room, there was ample space for limbs to unfold, stretch, and relax. Heating vents were at a distance as was the wood-burning stove that radiated tremendous warmth. With drop cloths in place to protect the wooden floors, the familiar sound of tires against the gravel sparked our excitement. Larry, his son, and my husband teamed once again to dismount the tree from the truck's bed, paused, and then huddled together hauling it a short distance up the steps to our home, and simultaneously lowered it to a soft landing resting upon the drop cloths. From there, it took only two strong backs to push the new arrival into its designated place. After receiving fully charted instructions from the learned professor of trees, our family continued to welcome our new member adorning it with decorations, love, and nourishment.

As the Christmas holiday passed, it was again time to call our friend Larry. Part of our family tradition of buying a living tree from Harmony Farms was having the knowledgeable professor perform its removal from the metal womb and carefully plan its placement into Mother Earth. Over the years, Larry typically arrived with one of his sons to help with the transplant. Some years, my husband accompanied him when his boys were not able to do so. Either way, before the procedure, a lengthy discussion took place as to where the tree would be placed. Having five acres to work with, this was a seemingly easy task, but there were many factors to consider. The soil needed to be void of larger rocks, of intruding roots, and of excess run-off from slopes and crevices. The size and shape of surrounding plants and trees were also a consideration for future growth and expansion. Sun and wind exposure as well as avoiding areas that attracted large amounts of snowfall were also blended into the delicate equation. As a participant in these discussions, I knew that even with the best planning in place, Nature would certainly have Her say in it—whether to accept or reject the transplant. Or perhaps Mother Nature would choose to test its endurance over time, seeing if the tree had within it the strength to fight its way through the adversities She imposed upon it. With Larry's expertise and years of experience, a decision for placement was made. And although there are never any guarantees, we all trusted in the process and in the knowledge that guided our decision. Only time would tell if the tree would find its way.

* * *

As the sun moved slowly to the west, the previously protective shadows from the trellis gave way to the warm rays caressing my face. Within a few minutes, their intensity brought discomfort. I shifted my chair under the stucco overhang and nearer to the friendly fountain. The splashing sounds lightened my spirit, allowing for rational thought to surface. Remembering the tradition of planting our living Christmas trees, I methodically recounted the lessons, searching for what I had learned and what I had overlooked.

First, Larry taught us about the delicacy of choosing a specific placement for transplanting our living trees. Two important factors were timing and spatial distancing. Timing involved the tree's readiness for removal from its container; it required that the tree was to be freed from its imposed metal constraint within a couple of weeks after the Christmas holidays. A delay could bring about root damage, dryness, or decay, and thus endanger its chances of survival. Equally important to the success of the transplant were the considerations for spatial distancing. Recalling the numerous factors of exposure to the elements, the demands from neighboring plant-life, and the implications for landscape variances, I was reminded of how difficult but imperative it was to provide a nurturing placement for the new transplant while still distancing it from long-standing adversaries.

As I thought about the past year, I recalled the elements of timing and spatial distancing that I believed I had carefully implemented into my life. When the feelings of self-doubt fostered by regression overcame me, when I felt I could no longer breathe, or when shame hung over me like a dark cloud, I would escape my betrayal environment, at least for short periods of time. Leaving the toxic container of valley fumes, I returned to the ponderosa pines which infused my increasingly shallow spirit with clean crisp air and provided a much-needed respite for a battered mind. The distance gave me time for my way of being to find its roots and revive them. As I began to feel reinvigorated and more alive, I promised myself that upon returning to hostile soil, I would work harder at protecting myself by implementing healthy boundaries and strategies. However, as is so common with relapse, when we re-enter territory that is not conducive to our wellbeing, the newly discovered and re-proclaimed promises dissipate more and more rapidly, leaving us more vulnerable than before. Although I felt

I had worked hard on this lesson by crafting protective time and space into my routine, I still felt responsible for putting myself at such risk.

Another important factor in the selection process of placement was respecting the integrity of the tree while at the same time honoring its need for familiarity. With this lesson, Larry taught us how important it was to give the young tree its independence and autonomy while at the same time keeping it tethered to the nutrients, which nourished its growth, and with the foundations which best supported it. Thus, although there was ample land from which to choose in the transplanting of the living trees, we consistently planted them near to mature pines whose longevity bore witness to healthy soil and to favorable conditions. The young trees, although vulnerable, also drew strength from the seasoned adult plants towering above and around them.

As I thought about this lesson of tethering oneself to objects of familiarity and of persons of support, I felt strong in this area as well. After moving into a new home mid-summer of 2008, I worked hard at creating an environment that would filter out the harmful triggers and distance me from poisonous sources of regression. Selecting earth-colored tones to paint the entire house brought in a sense of Nature's calm and beauty. Unpacking the myriad of ceramic, wooden, and metal animals I had collected over the years and strategically placing them on dark stained tables and silky white mantels teased the climate with a false memory of mountain life and drew me to a quieter place within. Large Native American feathered baskets were tucked into corners and brightly colored oil paintings from a well-known Cherokee artist adorned our walls. My favorite— an Indian warrior in full headdress riding a wild buffalo heading for battle— filled our living room with a courageous and confident spirit. A smaller one—a stately, lone Native Chief with long flowing grey hair standing among a grove of black pines and staring toward a mountain peak nestled in pinkish skies— provided a source of peaceful purpose and a sound serenity. Just outside, a statuesque pine-carved Bullwinkle-like moose, which greeted visitors at our mountain home, made the journey with us and kept me company on the back patio. Working hard to replicate the familiarity of our prior dwelling, I felt my roots were searching for and tethering themselves to the sources of renewal to which I had become accustomed. Unfortunately, when we place ourselves in highly unhealthy environments, even implementing numerous forces of familiarity or making sincere efforts at replicating surroundings that ensure a sense of safety and wellbeing are not enough to ward off or to arrest relapse.

The more I thought about the importance of this lesson, I realized that I had greatly misjudged my choice of transplant placement. And my deliberate and careful creation of a healing nurturing home as well as my attempts to tether myself to healthy influences were no match to the adversarial forces at play. Everywhere I turned in order to position myself in a place of nourishment, I came face-to-face with another toxin—a memory, a flashback, or a nightmare.

In order to survive and block out the pain, I overcommitted in every arena of my life. Doing more, doing for anyone who needed it, doing whatever it took to help or heal others, and doing very little for me became my way of rooting myself into the hostile territory. Forfeiting the lesson on tethering, my residual inner sources of renewal diminished and disappeared. On occasion and after a period of turmoil, attempts were made to adjust the borders of the transplant and to replenish the soil with an assortment of familiar nutrients, but their tenure was short lived. Without the support systems in place or the necessary resources to make up for basic deficiencies, my regression increased and the shame of it intensified. How easily I had forgotten that whenever or wherever there is a weak link in the recovering chain or a fissure in its path, relapse will not only move in, but it will take over.

Hearing the soft rippling of the waterfall, I grieved. Tears streamed down my face as I once again felt self-blame add its weight to the internal equation of regression into unhealthy ways of being. By slipping back into my old codependent behaviors and by neglecting the sound practices and principles of recovering, I had lost sight of one of Nature's most essential teachings. What had anchored me previously was continuing to slip away and I was scared. And now, as hard as I was fighting, I was losing more of myself every day. While mourning the present, my mind went back to Nature and to the Christmas Trees we planted. I thought of the year I watched one of our living trees die. It was slow and it broke my heart. Although many attempts were made to revive it, it could not withstand the forces fighting against it. When it was time to remove it, the needles were brown and brittle and the trunk dry. Unearthing it, I saw that the roots were mangled and meshed together in a crusty ball. It appeared as though they never had a chance at life, strangled before they could take a breath.

With each new day, I too felt it was becoming harder and harder to breathe. As my chest tightened and my lungs longed for fresh air, a few haunting questions filled my mind. "What possible good can come from this? Is there a reason for what I am going through? What can this relapse teach me that I didn't know before?" Inhaling the insanity of it all, a heavier shroud of shame covered me, smothering my roots and suffocating my being. If there was an answer, would I have the courage to find it? Was I willing to hear and was I ready to embrace what Nature would teach me next?

Chapter 4—Topics for Journaling & Recovery Work

1. As relapse moves in and takes over our being, we most often are filled with shame. Describe how shame feels for you and how it impacts your choices.

2. Another common feeling during relapse is one of "spiraling downward" or "spinning out of control." Describe that process for you. Also, discuss some of the "lifelines" (healthy or unhealthy), quick fixes, or diversions that you have embraced to assuage your guilt and pain. What have been the outcomes or results of choosing those healthy or unhealthy lifelines?

3. Putting oneself at risk is often a trigger or precursor into a period of relapse or regression into unhealthy patterns of behavior. As you think about your experience, discuss how neglecting or evading any one or more of these factors played a role:

    a. Timing—Did you know your levels of readiness or of weakness? Were you aware of your levels of recovering experience and the risks involved?
    b. Spatial distancing—Could you acknowledge the vulnerabilities and dangers in exposing yourself to unhealthy influences or environments?
    c. Tethering—Did you connect yourself to supportive people and places such as counselors, therapists, sponsors, recovering or support groups and programs, and/or other healthy, experienced mentors or professionals?

The Second Wind—Facing North

"Dear North, you are the direction of my spirit,
the direction of caution and great darkness,
the giver of winter, of phantoms,
of the snow that covers us in oneness."

—Kent Nerburn

Five—Fissure in the Soil

Fall 2010

In the fall of the third year away from the mountains, I arranged for an opportunity to visit the desert in Southern California where I had worked for many years. Looking forward to the fundraising event I was helping to sponsor gave me a much needed reprieve from the constraining forces of the valley environment. In fact, each time I made the drive, I noted that just about one hour beyond the outskirts of town and once over the first clustering of stunted hillsides, my mind cleared and my body felt lighter. My breathing slowed as the tight grip around my lungs loosened. The seven-hour drive down the vast interstate also gave me time to think and to reflect. Pulling away from farm-filled land, merging onto the truck-infested lanes, and focusing on the never-ending black pavement before me, I felt my brain settle into its analytical mode. With the inner insanity of the past many months gnawing at my consciousness, I began exploring the restraints of relapse—the trappings which contain us in our descent from recovery.

One of the restraints of relapse is wearing a mask of disguise. It is a mask that prevents others from seeing the turmoil that is wreaking havoc within; however, its adornment requires tremendous energy. As much as I was hurting, it was more important to me that others not see me as weak, or incapable, or vulnerable. Thus, my mask consisted of displaying a false self, not being authentic or real with who I was or what I was going through. Thinking about this concept made me realize that portraying myself in this manner is not only depleting to one's inner worth, but is also a form of betraying oneself.

As I continued driving, I thought about a second restraint of relapse—the mask of detachment. Wearing this mask allows an individual to insulate and to isolate the self from all voices of truth. It is one that feels protective in nature, but in reality, it is extremely dangerous. Whether the voices of truth consist of advice from trusted friends or family, or support from health care advocates, or from one's subconscious nudging, this restraint keeps us from connecting with healing and healthy realities. Although I felt that I was very much in touch with the truths around me and within me and that I needed to protect myself from unhealthy influences, I also knew that I was insulated from my usual support systems. My dearest, closest friends, with whom I trusted my authentic self, were living far away; my former therapist as well as several professional colleagues, with whom I often sought counsel, were also many miles away; and certainly the environmental connections from which I drew support were also out of reach. And thus, there were times when I felt extremely isolated and alone in my pain. Feeling my hand loosen a bit on the steering wheel, I realized it felt comforting to sort through these trappings and to understand their hold on me.

After driving several hours, I noticed the first of several mountain ranges. With many miles left to go, my thoughts returned to another restraint of relapse—the mask of denial. It is a mask that prevents one from being open to and aware of the triggers, or warnings, or other deeper issues that are fueling the downward spiral. Wearing this mask, too, requires tremendous energy. In order to repress our understanding of the causal factors of our behaviors or remove responsibility for their consequences, relapse demands a return to the same unhealthy behaviors that fuel our disease or that we acquire new destructive behaviors to camouflage our disorder. Part of the insidiousness of relapse is that none of these maladaptive efforts can be maintained or sustained even though we may invest tremendous energy into them. And, until we are ready and willing to break through the denial, we will never be able to reach our full potential for recovering. As I reflected on this concept, I wondered why I was not paying more attention to this mask and how it was impacting me. For over two years, I was struggling and fighting against an opponent that was relentless. As I began to climb the first large mountain, I questioned myself. Was there something I was repressing? What was it that I was denying?

My attention shifted slightly as I entered into the frantic pace of the steep grade dodging vehicles as they were swerving and vying for prime positions on the highway. I found a lane suited for my speed which allowed me to move with efficiency but also permitted me to enjoy the green rolling mountains flanked with jagged rocky cliffs. While remaining cautious and careful in my driving, my mind wandered into Nature's classroom. This time I was here not only for Her teachings, but I was ready to stop running from or denying any difficult truths.

*   *   *

Nature truly is patient with us. When we enter into a relationship with Her, it seems odd to me that we are often surprised or alarmed that there are consequences to the human expectations we impose upon Her. As much as our family respected the natural rights of the grounds we called our home, we, too, were often challenged by the stubbornness and willfulness of our Mother Earth. On some occasions, the crises at hand were averted; in other instances, working together brought mutual reward. And many times, Nature took the upper hand and had Her way. Regardless of the outcome, over the years living on the mountain, we learned to live in harmony with Her by listening to the messages and learning from the warnings She sent our way.

Living at an elevation of about 4500 feet, we were blessed to experience just enough snowfall throughout the winter season to remain joyful about its presence. Typically, a storm would pass through and grace us with a few inches of soft powder. The whipped substance might stay for a day or even two, but within a short period of time thereafter, the milky patches would secretly disappear into the soil below. There were a number of years when colder air streams visited us, leaving a heavy white footprint of Nature's force and power.

On these occasions, it was mandatory to awake and to ready our family for an even earlier departure than usual to navigate safely down the mountain road.

It was a day or two after one of our bountiful snowfalls that my husband, daughter, and I all arose in the dark morning hours to begin our journey to our respective jobs and to school. Stepping outside in the brisk mountain air, my husband surveyed the degree of icy snow and peered into the black night, blindly assessing the road conditions. As usual, he would leave first marking our way with his tire tracks and when possible, calling us with important information. With cell phone reception almost non-existent, once my daughter and I left our home, we were on our own. As I learned on many mornings, driving on snow or ice, or both, especially down a windy dangerously steep road, demanded a high degree of concentration, confidence, and courage. Possessing all three along with years of experience, I cautiously made my way from our home street to the mountain highway. The sun started to peer over the nearby eastern range and little streams of water slid down the rocky banks and onto the pavement. I knew what this meant and I slowed the speed of the car. On the still shady parts of the black asphalt, thin sheets of clear water pooled and froze. I cautiously continued as I approached the most difficult twists and turns anticipating the black ice that lay hidden in the shadows.

Without warning, the car slid and I reflexively and mistakenly pressed the brakes. The car spun rapidly, making a ninety-degree turn and crashing into a southern section of the rocky hillside bordering the ice-way. After the front of the car hit the boulders at full speed, we ricocheted backwards and bolted into the mountain wall on the opposing side of the highway. Hearing the thud of my daughter's head against the side window, I grabbed her with my right arm, making certain she was belted in. All of a sudden, the car made one last jolt and we landed right in the middle of the highway, like a smashed accordion thrown onto a lonely dance floor. Quickly checking my daughter for injuries, I also glanced into the rear view mirror, fearful of other approaching vehicles. To my horror, several more cars were being ambushed by the black, shiny, frozen sheets and were smashing into the rocks and into one another. I grabbed my daughter and we exited our car immediately so as to avoid any oncoming traffic from around the blind curve ahead. As we huddled together by the side of the mountain, I could feel her trembling and shaking. I held her tightly and was able to determine that aside from the small bump on her head, she was alright. Within seconds, people were jumping from their cars, checking on one another, and making the necessary calls for help.

Within a couple of hours, our crushed car was towed to a mechanic's garage in a nearby small mountain community, and my daughter and I waited for my husband at a familiar café not far from our home. As I sat cuddling my little girl and sipped on my hot chocolate, I thought of how incredibly fortunate we were. And, I couldn't help but feel a deep sense of gratitude as well. Playing *back the accident in my mind, it was clear that the mountain's posture saved us both. Along the stretch where I hit the black ice, each side of the highway was mostly flanked by steep cliffs with dangerous drops. However, in the exact location where I lost control, Nature reached out Her rocky arms, blocking our fall on both sides and pushing us back into Her safe embrace. There is comfort in knowing that in times of crises or upheaval, the sources that we trust to protect and guard us are often right in front of us. Sometimes, when we are struggling through a period of relapse or of regression, we don't see them or acknowledge them; but they are there. That day, Nature clearly reminded me of Her loyal presence.*

As the days passed and I continued to replay the accident over and over, the magnitude of what happened began to sink in and I felt humbled by another cautionary message. Having driven this mountain road hundreds and hundreds of times and in all kinds of conditions, I relied upon the years of experience to guide my way. I didn't doubt or question what I knew; at the same time, I felt that I should have handled the road differently. Thinking about what could have happened, tremendous anxiety and fear started to take hold of me. Rehearsing the could haves, should haves, and would haves produced feelings of guilt and over-responsibility. But, as time went by, I was able to release the negative forces that were diminishing the waves of gratitude and appreciation for Nature's life lessons. In letting go and in forgiving myself, I was reminded that regardless of the degree of experience or healing that we may carry with us, there is never any way of fully preparing for what may lie ahead. Remaining aware of our humanity allows us to move forward in confidence while maintaining a healthy humility which keeps us open to further exploration, knowledge, and growth.

* * *

Once over the mountain range and beyond the Greater Los Angeles area, I dropped down into the desert landscape. Entering into a field of cities sprinkled across the desert floor, I drove swiftly and without distraction down the empty interstate. I took in a few deep breaths and relaxed in the wisdom of Nature's lessons. Recalling these teachings reminded me there are lessons that continually need to be revisited and reworked. At the same time, I reminded myself that when we enter into a phase of relapse, our minds are bombarded with toxic intrusive messages that blind us to our hard-earned truths. It is often difficult if not impossible to recognize the loss of our current healing reality, to admit we have fallen short, and to begin the process of forgiving—not just of ourselves but of others as well.

As I continued driving for several miles, I passed acres upon acres of sterile windmills, which lined the desert floor and disappeared into the folds of the mountain range. Recalling the recent months of regression into painful patterns, I also reminded myself that recovering is never done. I shifted my position in the driver's seat, and yet, I still felt uneasy. I quietly asked myself, "Was there something that was unfinished?" My mind kept going back to the mask of denial and how its restraints keep us from reaching our healing potential. I thought about my choices and how they were playing a part in my relapse. I was continuing to tackle more responsibility in work areas and to take care of the needs of others around me. In futile attempts to assuage my internal erosion, the more I kept filling the widening crevice inside me with personal and professional obligations, the more burdened and powerless I felt. Contrary to the false sense of sanity that denial messages send us, when we don't pay attention to the warning signs, or when we think we can do it our way or on our own, we actually make ourselves the most vulnerable. And we set ourselves up for prolonged pain. Although I was fighting against external betrayal forces, the hurt buried inside of me was becoming more easily triggered. As I kept pushing it down, it resisted and I felt the poisonous fumes filling up within me, filtering through my lungs, and stretching up into my throat. Each day was becoming harder and harder to catch my breath.

My thoughts returned fully to my driving as I exited the freeway. A few miles into a lovely protective cove of the desert, I arrived at my destination—an extraordinarily designed French Chateau nestled on sprawling green lawns bordering an exquisite lake. This inn was one of the desert's best kept secrets, and I quickly checked in and unpacked my belongings. My room—*Safari*—was a favorite among all the carefully detailed and decorated choices. With its elephant and giraffe figurines accented with leopard linens and tiger prints, the room transported me to a place of peace.

Tired after the long drive, I changed into some comfortable clothes. I opened the French doors from this second story room that led out to a quaint terrace. A cool breeze brushed in from the pristine lake and the sounds of shooting water from a massive center lake fountain reverberated throughout the otherwise tranquil setting. Returning to the dark, solid wood, four-poster bed with silky white mosquito netting delicately draping its corners, I lay down and rested my eyes. Closing my eyes and relaxing my body, I took in several deep breaths. My mind was continuing to replay the lessons on denial; I couldn't seem to let go of it. However, listening to the splashing sounds in the background proved comforting and calming. Pushing myself to be open and aware to what Nature wanted to teach me, I thought back to one of Her most brutally truth-filled tales.

* * *

Our home was perched on the side of a steep hill. Although Nature had provided a flat building pad for our man-made nest, a relatively short distance separated it from the nests high above used by our animal neighbors. Snuggled up against its hulk-like stance, our house was protected from various dangers by the rocky, sparsely-filled stocky mountain; and yet, the very same mound proved a constant source of concern. With each and every heavy rain storm, run-off filled with a sandy substance and thousands of tiny rocks deposited itself on the back decking. After one downpour where several inches of dirt crept toward our sliding glass doors, a retaining wall was constructed along with an elaborate drainage system that would carry the debris to the west side of the hill, where it was redirected. At times, the reconstruction served its purpose; however, during prolonged thunderstorms, the pipes were buried and the rushing streams created their own escape route. No matter how hard my husband worked to remedy the problem, Nature remained resistant and continued to leave her sunken imprint down the western side of our hill. Over time, the tiny fissure in the soil where the water flowed began to widen and deepen. After one particularly rainy season, the fissure slowly crawled towards our home and then opened its jaws as though it were going to devour it.

Alarmed by the proximity and size of the cave-like crevice, we took immediate steps to fill in the ominous cracks until appropriate measures could be taken. Several contractors recommended filling in the fissure with cement, making a permanent passageway for the run-away waters. Not wanting to strap a man-made cast onto Nature's side, we decided to create a more natural solution. After securing some eco-friendly tarp material, my husband and I carefully measured, cut, and laid the gauze onto the deep open wound. Then, over a couple of days, we gathered and carried large rocks and small boulders to the surgical site. Starting at the bottom of the pre-emptive incision, we placed the various stone transplants into the fissure, making sure each one fit securely and solidly. Working from dawn to dusk for two more days, we scaled the slippery hill, filling in every gap and adding extra layers of rocks where needed. At times, the pressure of the foreign substances would actually cause the wound to widen and other fissures would need to be cauterized.

By the end of the weekend, my husband and I were exhausted but relieved. The danger was averted while still honoring Nature's integrity and beauty. Over the ensuing seasons, the man-made implant protected the house from further injury. And yet, it had its limitations. When the rains hit hard and the waters weighed heavily on the boulders, the fissure deepened, little by little. And when the rushing streams overflowed onto the naked soil, newer fissures opened, creating more areas of concern. Although we continued to monitor any changes or movements, we knew that someday a more permanent remedy would need to be implemented. And while we knew that a more comprehensive procedure would be less attractive, would create more of a disturbance to the natural flow of the land, and would be much more costly, we also knew there was no other way to make it right.

*   *   *

As I lay listening to the fountain waters and thinking of the fissure in the soil, warm tears rolled down my face. After two years of living in my betrayal environment, I knew I was losing myself. The fissure of pain inside of me was deepening and widening. Every time I took on another task, helped another person, performed another role, I added a boulder onto the sinking crevice. On the outside, it appeared as though the waters were running smoothly down the bedrocks of responsibilities that I had created. On the inside, the weight of rock-pile was pulling me down, anchoring me in despair. And when the painful triggers of the past overwhelmed me, my emotions swirled and erupted, causing fissures to surface in other parts of my being. Responding in a reactive way, thinking defensively, and being overly sensitive that others viewed me in a critical light were foreign behaviors that I had long since abandoned. Their return frustrated me and brought me additional embarrassment and shame. My healed, peace-filled way of being was slipping away and I grieved for it. I wondered if I would ever be able to get it back. As I slowly shifted and nestled myself into the soft animal print throws and pillows that filled the bed, my mind once again drifted back to our mountain home.

As I continued to visualize the fissure which endangered our home and recall how difficult it was to remedy the problem, I thought of the underlying condition of the soil. It was light and porous; it moved like the sand on the beach when a wave washes over it. There was no way that over time it could endure the raging waters that flowed over it, let alone sustain the weight of the boulders placed upon it. Trusting my healing experiences, I thought about my underlying condition as well. Yes, I knew my inner soil was light and porous, but it was also strong. I had experienced trauma, and I had tenderly and courageously treated that wound years ago. But was there more that I was not seeing or sensing? Was my inner fissure composed of sharp fragments of forgotten pain that were getting pushed deeper into my being against the weight of betrayal's boulders? Was I ready to start removing the heavy rocks lodged in my deepening crevice? Was I willing to face what I might find?

Whatever I would decide, I knew the process would not be easy; I knew the emotional costs would be high. Exploring causation and arresting relapse always is. Most importantly, I knew that by embracing recovering, I must interrupt and disrupt the natural flow of denial. It was time to remove this mask of relapse; it was time to let go of its hold on my being. As I looked around the room and directly into the eyes of the African animals staring at me from the fireplace mantle and from the wooden cubbies in every corner, the fear within me started to subside. Face to face with Nature, the lesson in front of me was mine for the taking.

Chapter 5—Topics for Journaling & Recovery Work

1. In this chapter, we were reminded of the "restraints of relapse". I talked about them in the form of "masks" because when we enter into a period of relapse or regression, we do not live "in truth". With each or all of your masks, describe how they played a part in creating a life of lies and in robbing you of your truths.

    a. Mask of Disguise—How do you present the "false"? How do you act when you are pretending that your life is fine? What lies do you tell yourself or others? What unhealthy behaviors do you return to or acquire in order to hide your decline into relapse?

    b. Mask of Detachment—As soon as you start slipping into relapse or regression, what healthy or healing realities do you let go of first? What do you stop doing that supports your recovery? Whom do you avoid and why? What else do you do to isolate yourself from the truth?

    c. Mask of Denial—What lies do you tell yourself that prevent you from facing triggers, warning signs, or deeper issues? What excuses do you give for your relapse? Whom do you blame or hold responsible for your relapse or "bad lot in life", instead of looking at yourself? How does it feel when you negate your real or authentic self? How do you know when you are truly betraying yourself and your recovering work? Describe how that feels for you.

2. Once we have broken through the restraints of relapse, especially the mask of denial, we position ourselves in a place of awakening and we begin to acknowledge our truths. By practicing honesty, with ourselves and with others, we begin the healing process. As we begin to peel away the masks and uncover the "fissures in our soil", we may enter an extremely vulnerable and pain-filled state. Therefore, it is highly recommended to move through this process with the guidance of a trusted professional such as a therapist, counselor, sponsor, or recovering expert. As you do so, explore the following fissures, uncover the injury or harm they bring to you, and discover how they impact your healing journey.

a. Triggers

b. Chain of events leading to relapse; examination of weak links

c. Flashbacks, memories, dreams

d. Self-inventories

e. Crises, trauma, or abuse issues

f. Unhealthy, abusive, or violent relationships

g. Family of origin issues

h. Addictive or codependent behaviors

i. Other destructive patterns of behavior or thinking; other maladaptive behaviors or thought processes

As painful as this process can be, identifying and working through our fissures is essential in order to break through the realities of relapse and to unleash the shroud of shame it carries with it. If we are to reclaim ourselves, we must do this.

Six—Bark Beetles

Fall 2010

Over the next several days, I busied myself with fundraising activities as well as spending time with close friends. By the fourth day, I was looking forward to relaxing at the inn, simply enjoying the quiet and the solitude of the lovely chateau. With the weekend passed and with all of the remaining guests returning home, I had the miniature castle to myself. After sleeping in and then enjoying a leisurely breakfast, I sat outside with a cup of coffee. The patio off the luxurious sitting room was framed with tropical flowers and island-like plants. Large sloping green grounds surrounded the French chateau while statuesque palms provided privacy from neighboring homes. Beyond the lush lawns, the lake shimmered in the early morning sunlight and the lone fountain was hushed by human timers. Except for a few calls from Nature, all was still.

Finishing my coffee, I strolled over to a small cluster of palms and sat down on the grass. Leaning my head back on the uneven stem, I started thinking about my trip home and of what I needed to do when I returned. As I did so, my thoughts shifted back to the lesson from a few days previously—the flow of denial. As much as I wanted to reclaim myself, an inner tug-of-war was continuing to send mixed messages. I knew this was how denial worked, but it was still hard to fight against it. One part of me felt determined to do whatever it would take to tackle the fissures of truth within; the other part of me challenged that thinking with deception and lies. This is the insidiousness of denial. It is so easy to put our truths on hold or to denounce them when our brain is telling us that we should just give ourselves a little more time or that we have not been trying hard enough. Or, we believe that things are really not that bad, at least not in the moment. To add to our confusion, many times we place ourselves in unhealthy environments or with toxic influences where we can normalize our regression, at least temporarily. We also listen to the lies of others, who want to keep us in our state of relapse so as not to disturb the dynamics of relationships with them or to challenge their unhealthiness as well. This is the craziness of denial—the internal tug-of-war between truth and lie. Sanity rests in knowing that we have a choice; we can choose to honor our truths.

As I readjusted my position and leaned up against the palm trunk more closely, I could feel its sharp-crusted shell brace my body. Although it was slightly uncomfortable, its strength and sturdiness was awkwardly comforting. Nestling in just a bit more and hearing a crunching sound from the brittle fingernail-like protrusions, my thoughts went to Nature. Her next lesson was to be my most difficult to integrate into my journey; Her next lesson would guide me as I broke though the denial.

* * *

Nature's formidable presence tends to disguise the fragility within Her. Each species, animal or plant, carefully weaves together a tapestry of balance that both nurtures and tests Her existence. Unrelenting intruders as well as environmental shifts also impose their will upon Nature's resilient and yet tiring soul. Some catastrophes re-landscape the face of Her being, leaving Her barren and vulnerable. Other intrusions flaw Her appearance or destroy Her finely tuned inner workings. And still, Nature remains. And still, She teaches.

In the late 1990s, there were several years of extreme drought in our mountain area as well as in numerous parts of California. Although the concern over fire danger was always with us, a more significant threat began to descend upon the weakened pine forests that decorated the ground floor and tickled the skies above. The ominous sign first became present when the top needles of soaring pines started turning a reddish brown. At first it was just a few trees scattered here and there. And then, over a period of several months, a blanket of green forest turned into a blanket of red rust. As devastating as it was to witness the slow death of our plant neighbors, it was even more alarming to discover the cause—bark beetles.

Bark beetle adults are small, cylindrical, hard bodied insects about the size of a grain of rice. Most species are dark red, brown, or black. Because of their microscopic size, they can be viewed closely only under magnification. Their grotesque minute appearance is marked by enlarged club-like antennae and with heads that appear to be engulfed by their bodies. Bark beetles have strong jaws for chewing and their presence is typically first noted by the buckshot pattern of holes and by the dry boring dust that is apparent on the bark surface of infested branches or trunks. Once trees have become vulnerable because of lack of water or because hard winters have softened them, bark beetles are able to flourish and to expand their infestation. Using their back-hoe jaws, the beetles drill through the pine bark and dig a gallery in the wood where their eggs are laid. Deeply embedded into the interior being of the trees, the larvae are left to hatch. As they grow, the narrow larval mines expand and enlarged malignant birth chambers invade the pines' weakened wood. When the adults emerge, the plump whitish larvae eat the sweet, rich cambium layer that provides nutrients to the tree.

Advancing their aggressive onslaught, the deadly warriors fend off the potential for drowning from moving sap by injecting a fungus into the trees to arrest it. As the pines desperately fight back by emitting white resin into the beetle's drill holes, the attackers put out a hormone-based call for reinforcements and more beetles swarm the tree. Although there are occasions when the trees win and entomb their enemies, when there has been significant decline in the pines' stamina and strength, the once magnificent towers of the forest have trouble producing enough resin and they are overwhelmed. Without immediate and effective intervention to save the life of an infected tree, adult bark beetles may re-infest the same tree or disperse to attack susceptible trees elsewhere. Within a relatively short period of time, an entire forest can be lost.

Watching the canopy of green across the mountain skyline shifting to a reddish-brown sickened every homeowner. As we waited and watched for the inevitable spread into our susceptible ponderosa valley, I remember getting up each morning, peering out the windows of our home, and scouring the property for any signs of infestation. One day as I was out walking and studying the pines very closely, I noticed that one solitary statuesque tree situated on the west side of our home was in trouble. The needles at the very top of the tree were turning a light brownish color. I knew what this meant. The engraver beetles, which were known to our mountain area, attacked trees near the top of the stem, making it impossible to stop their invasion. The soaring pine appeared so strong, and yet, I was well aware that the years of drought and warmer winters had weakened its defenses and had produced ideal conditions for its betrayers to enter. As the weeks wore on, the reddish brown color descended onto the lower branches and needles. The limbs that were first infected died and their brittle bark broke free from the trunk, leaving small corpses on the ground below. During the ensuing months, the bark beetles relentlessly continued their advancement, burrowing deeply into the core of the massive trunk, producing more warriors, cutting off its source of nourishment, and infiltrating the remaining healthy areas. My family and I watched, helplessly, as the pine slowly suffocated and eventually succumbed. The bark beetles overwhelmed it. The betrayers won.

* * *

Recalling the lesson of the bark beetles was difficult; but then facing the truth of disease and dying is as well. I shifted my position against Nature's back support and found an indentation that proved more inviting. As I continued to think about the lone infested tree we lost on our property, I remembered how it died—slowly and from the inside out. Visualizing how the bark beetles bored mercilessly into the center of the tree, cutting off its life sources and strangling it, I knew that betrayal's beetles were doing the same to me. Lodged deeply within my core, they were managing to dig their way into the galleries of my being. Each day I was finding it harder and harder to catch my breath. Each day, the air I breathed seemed filled with toxins and the resins inside me could not entomb them. My spirit felt weighted down by the dry brittle fragments within me, and at times, I could feel them fall away, leaving me with less of myself than before.

Picturing those final days when the strong, soaring pine succumbed to a skeleton of broken brownish red branches, I knew that it was time for me to identify the species of betrayal that invaded my core and infested the chambers of my spirit. As quickly as I entertained this thought, my mind wanted to escape it. Denial reared its ugly force as fear ran through my arteries and shame filled my veins. Tears welled and spilled. For a moment, I simply shook. My thoughts resisted the lies and returned to the tortured tree and its legacy. Because we were willing to sacrifice that one precious tree, we were able to save those around it. And although the process was incredibly pain-filled, the only hope for new growth was to allow the tree to die, and then to remove all the decay, making certain no traces of infection were left behind.

Wiping my eyes and calming my being, I knew that I had to do the same. I knew that I could not give up or give in. Nature taught me long ago that resiliency is a finely blended outgrowth of devastation and courage. After all the years of hard work and healing I achieved, I needed to put aside the disappointment in myself for not being able to sustain that level of wellness within an environment that was contrary to its existence. I needed to let go of the embarrassment that although I was knowledgeable in the ways of betrayal, I was a weakened, vulnerable, lone tree fighting against the unforeseeable tests of

Nature and the changing conditions She brings with Her. And I needed to make whatever sacrifices were necessary to rid myself of the relentless warriors within who were out to destroy my way of being. If I was going to reclaim myself, there was no other choice. As I thought about what lay ahead, I slowly raised my head up and felt a fresh breeze gently caress my warm tear-stained face. Nature was with me. Her truths would clear the way.

Chapter 6—Topics for Journaling & Recovery Work

1. Just when we make the decision to start loving ourselves again and to move forward in our recovering process, our old self (the personality of lies) begins to plant seeds of doubt. We begin to question our decision to move forward in healthy ways and we minimize the unhealthiness we have been experiencing. It is indeed an inner battle of tug-of-war between what it true and what is false. Describe some of the ways that your old self tests you and tricks you. Identify them and explain how they weave their way into ways of thinking and behaving, all in an attempt to sabotage your recovering.

2. During a period of relapse or of regression, we also experience feelings of disappointment and embarrassment in not living up to our healing potential. We have let ourselves down and we have let others down. How have these feelings or others played a role in sustaining your relapse or in discouraging you to move forward in wellness?

3. Because we are weakened and tempted by so many different sources in our environments, we often need to make difficult choices to remove or distance ourselves from those toxic influences. What sacrifices have you made or are you willing to make in order to create positive change and support a healthy recovering process?

The Third Wind—Facing East

"To you, the east, the direction of the sunrise,
where hope is born and every day begins anew."

—Kent Nerburn

Seven—Peeling Away the Bark

Late Fall 2010—Winter 2011

For several weeks after returning home, I kept myself busy with professional obligations and personal commitments. However, during this time, I continually revisited my insights and reflections on relapse and the lessons of the bark beetles. While staying at the French chateau, I made a choice to honor my truths; now it was time to act upon that decision. From my work with clients and in my own recovering, I knew that this was an extremely vulnerable position. Denial does not like to rest; its lies are ready and willing to sabotage truth at every turn.

One morning while enjoying a cup of coffee in my home office and getting ready to do some writing, I started reading through some old notations on the topic of betrayal. I surprised myself that I had kept these scribblings tucked away among other current works. Perusing these past case studies where I had made generalized clinical notations regarding the issue of relapse or regression into unhealthy addictions, or behaviors, or relationships, I noted the various examples of how clients broke through their denial and began reclaiming themselves. This reminded me of the importance of conducting a fearless inventory of one's areas of vulnerability, of weakness, and of injury. Whether it is a physical, emotional, psychological, or environmental trigger, or whether it is involvement in unhealthy relationships or toxic influences, or if it is deeply embedded injustice, we each must acknowledge them and act upon their removal. Breaking through the denial within relapse or regression begins with being honest with oneself and being willing to face what one finds. Although this work is not easy, it is necessary.

As I continued to browse through my notes, I thought of my own recovering journey and that of many clients. Sometimes there are wounds buried deeply within one's being that trigger and/or that sustain an episode of relapse or a state of regression. Many times we do not know they are there; many times we know something is terribly wrong, but we don't know why or how to address it. What most of us need at this point is someone with trusted experience and integrity to help us find our way. Putting aside my notations, I thought of the many clients I worked with who conducted their fearless inventories with courage and dignity. I reminded myself of how we tenderly peeled away layers of injury and gently addressed their pain within. Recalling their journeys tugged at my heart and I was humbled by their healing experiences and their courage. My mind struggled and then wavered for a moment; then it reluctantly opened itself to Nature's most poignant and painful lesson.

* * *

Once Nature has endured an injury or an injustice, there is typically controversy about how, if at all, to heal or to correct that misfortune. Varying interests certainly play a role in the decisions of how and when to move forward with an intervention or a plan. Over the years living in the mountains, I bore witness to conflicting opinions and viewpoints. And although there was often indifference that called for "letting Her be", or for "letting Nature take Her own course", there were many inhabitants who demanded that conscientious and qualified attention be given to Her rescue and recovery. Either way, Nature waited patiently. And whether treatments were imposed upon Her or whether She was left to fend for Herself, it was with time that Her wounds healed and mended or that the infection was sustained and spread. And so was the case with the bark beetles.

After several years of vast infestation and devastation, in the early 2000s, a decision was finally made by the powers-that-be to remove the malignant invader that was destroying a national forest. A multitude of rescuers arrived on the scene of San Bernardino's monumental graveyard. Thousands of brownish headstones still rose up to meet the heavens while rotting corpses lay in piles on the ground floor. Massive bulldozers with giant jaws scooped up the remains and carried them off-site to mill them properly. Other machines roared along the steep hillsides like computer-animated monsters ripping out entire trunks and loading them onto train-like flat beds awaiting their transport. Air support was called upon as helicopters hovered high above rocky peaks lowering their equipment, grabbing hold of skeletal remains and hoisting them up and then onto waiting trucks. Brave, well-trained men and women worked tirelessly through the spring, summer, and fall months attacking the bark beetle malignancy that had spread like wildfire. With an aggressive frontal assault that lasted not just months but years, the bark beetle-infested trees were extricated, leaving the betrayers without host homes for their re-entry or without any opportunity to invade healthy trees.

Although removal of the dead and deceased pines was paramount to the survival of the forest, the skilled professionals carefully examined surrounding living trees for any signs of the microscopic invaders. This procedure, although time-consuming, saved the remaining trees. The labor intensive process could be done by hand or mechanically. If a tree was suspect to infection, the surgeon would precisely and gingerly peel away the bark just enough to expose the larvae developing underneath. All bark that was concealing betrayers must be removed; neglecting any hidden enemies would endanger the entire tree and its neighbors. By peeling away the bark, the larvae became exposed to unfavorable conditions which caused them to dehydrate, starve, and eventually die. With the enemy completely eradicated, the tree was freed from the strangulation within and its nutrients once again flowed without interruption. Now, there was hope for its renewal.

* * *

As my thoughts returned to the present, I felt an uneasiness within me. There was more to this lesson—a critical piece that almost cost the forest her life. I scoured my mind searching for Nature's central message. Her truth surfaced. With an uncomfortable stillness, I remembered how the experts as well as the homeowners all desperately hoped that Nature could fight off the bark beetles on her own. Precious time was lost as she proved ill-matched to the army that descended upon her. By the time reinforcements and rescuers were called in, it was almost too late. But, there was no question; the skilled surgeons saved her. As I closed my eyes and visualized the lush green canopy that once again graced the mountainous land, I recalled how Her majesty and magnificence was balanced out by her fragility and frailty. I was reminded that even the strongest of cores can succumb to overwhelming contagions. I opened my eyes and leaned back on the sofa. I took in a deep breath and exhaled slowly. It was time to conduct my inventory; it was time to peel away the layers of injury. Most importantly, there was no more time to waste trying to fight off the infestation alone. I knew I needed a skilled professional to guide my way.

I spent the next several days searching for an individual in whom I would place my trust and my truths. After several calls and with brief conversations, I found myself in the presence of a warm, nurturing, wise woman. Her soft demeanor immediately comforted my spirit as did the earth-toned décor that filled the room. As we sat and talked, I shared my story of recovering and of regression. I disclosed the excitement, anticipation, and strength with which I re-entered my betrayal environment, and I painfully admitted to the shame, guilt, and self-blame for the eroded and weakened place from which I now navigated. I wept and cringed as I said the words, "The worst part is that I betrayed myself. I let myself down. I thought I could remain true to myself and all that I had become. And now, all of it is gone. All of it is lost."

As weeks passed and our sessions continued, I shared more of my background and history. My compassionate mother-figure allowed me to take the lead, giving me space and time for trust to build. As we talked about the drought in my life and the variables that had primed and sustained that weakened state, I began to ease up on myself and even forgive myself for falling short. It felt good to cut off and let go of those brittle branches of self-loathing and self-pitying; at the same time, it was important to own my responsibilities and decisions in healthy and balanced ways. I was starting to experience a level of relief and renewal. And yet, the insightful healer knew there was more.

Just as the bark was painstakingly removed from the beetle-infested trees, my gifted guide started to pull away tenderly at the layers of hardened tissue that protected the diseased larvae within. With each peeling came the exposure of a galley buried within my core. As we ventured together into the tunnels, I was forced to come face to face with my betrayers. As I looked inside and saw the ugliness, I could not breathe. My body ached and my mind swirled. I wept and I choked. My tender counselor comforted me and calmed me. I frightfully returned my focus to the larvae facing me. It was an oversized, grotesque female—a supposed friend who became a violator.

The force of the attack surged though my memory like a tsunami sweeping through unsuspecting territory. Tears flowed freely and I grieved aloud. The unveiling sent a sharp sting deep into my being that reverberated for several minutes. My mother-like figure held my wounded soul and nurtured it with her words of understanding and unconditional regard. Taking time to pause and release, together we pulled away a few pieces of remaining bark, making certain no larvae were hidden elsewhere. As the burning sting subsided, I could feel the gallery of pain within me lessen and gently close. Warm tears caressed my cheeks as a renewing realization entered my being. Stripped from their protective bark of denial and exposed to the elements of healing, the dehydrated, poisonous larvae had starved, shriveled up, and died.

As our sessions continued, my skilled companion assisted me as we peeled away other pieces of bark, checking for vulnerable areas of infestation or of further infection. Although there were several places of minor injury, nothing significant surfaced. What we did uncover were old galleries filled with dead larvae, sometimes so many that they were piled on top of one another. Carefully cleaning out the scar-filled tunnels, I realized that there were so many years where I felt that I had not been protected from harm or that I was left alone to fend for myself. My thoughts went to the trees that suffered needlessly for so many years while knowledgeable bystanders thought that Nature could take care of herself and that She would be ok. I recalled thoughts of how it was almost too late to save the forest because of the tug-of-war between the costs of paying attention and the ease of pretending what was not. I remembered that although so many mountain inhabitants knew in their guts of the eminent and inherent danger from the bark beetles, their lives were filled with busyness and there simply wasn't time to pay attention or to care.

As I journeyed through the galleries with my mother guide, my truth mirrored that of the decaying forest. Each layer of dead larvae represented a period of time that I felt vulnerable and weakened on some level. And, without the protection and validation I felt I deserved, I lost my voice and I turned inward. Throughout the years, as unfavorable conditions provided host homes for additional larvae to produce feelings of inadequacy and isolation, I wondered if anyone noticed the danger I was in. I wondered if anyone would come and rescue me. Mostly, I wondered if I mattered. I longed for someone—anyone—to listen to me, to believe me, and to protect me. As I cleaned out the tunnels diligently removing any remnants of skeletal remains, I grieved for the time that was lost—not just the time lost waiting for the rescuers to come, but for the time the betrayers had with which to hold me hostage. It was time now to uproot it all and to remove it. As I visualized how the monstrous jaws of the backhoes cleared out the brown brittle trees, I dug even more deeply to scoop up the decayed roots of shame and blame. And as I recalled how the helicopters hoisted up the broken brown trunks carrying them far away, I too pictured the breezes in my mind sweeping up the crusty carcasses depositing them high into the skies. I felt them drift away. Finally, I was free to breathe once again.

As I continued working with my compassionate guide, I was reminded that investing into my wellbeing meant making it a priority. And, for the time being as I remained in an environment that was not filled with the nutrients that fed and nourished me, I needed to reinstitute some of the same controls I utilized in previous healing seasons as well as embrace stronger boundaries and build protective spaces around me. Thinking back on the lesson in the forest, I remembered that once the crises of the bark beetle infestation subsided due to the successful interventions, other measures were put into place. Although it was not possible to prevent another occurrence, there were cultural, biological, behavioral, and chemical controls that could be implemented in order to protect the forest. What most of us learned from the bark beetle tragedy was that cost of investing into protective measures would always pale to the pricey consequences of neglect. I was relearning how valuable that lesson was.

Although my sessions continued for the next several months, their urgency subsided and I found myself back into a rhythm and harmony of renewal. The heavy blankets of shame and self-blame that smother us during relapse or regression were tossed aside and the refreshing sheets of recovering returned and brought much comfort. Recalling past clients who reclaimed their lives after relapse and thinking about my own journey, the humanity of it all humbled me once again. Recognizing that there are many defense mechanisms that get in our way and cloud our thinking, our most formidable opponent in fighting relapse is our own ego—our over-reliance on self. We listen to our lies and we believe them. We also welcome the lies of others in order to validate our choices. We become masters at negating our truths. Over time and as our lives continue to reel out of control, we begin to loathe ourselves for failing and we waste time floundering in a pool of self-pity. Smothered by the masks of relapse, what we often don't realize is that the failure itself provides the fertile ground from which to begin again. By discarding those masks, facing our truths, and remaining open to sources of integrity, we can learn from our experiences. It is so often the lessons learned from our most painful experiences which strengthen us and guide us in our healing paths ahead. They are ours for the taking.

While driving home after my therapy session and reminding myself of that truth, I thought about my current healing reality. It was essential that I remain open to and aware of my environment and its influences upon my being. Thinking about the lessons of the bark beetle infestation, my mind quickly returned to the lone tree by our house that became so diseased and damaged that her limbs began to droop and then to break. I remembered that although the decision to remove the tree was extremely difficult, we eventually had to sacrifice it in order to save the others on our property from the rampant infection spreading throughout the mountain. I thought of everything I had worked on in order to eradicate and extricate the disease within, and how for the first time in almost three years I was able to breathe freely and without fear. And yet, I knew I was not done. I knew that in order to safeguard the state of wellness I achieved, my budding truths were not to be sacrificed for anyone or anything. Claiming them, protecting them, and honoring them were critical to their growth and thus to my recovering. Although the lone tree did not survive, her legacy served me well.

Chapter 7—Topics for Journaling & Recovery Work

1. As we discussed in Chapter Five—Fissure In The Soil—Chapter Seven is also about facing and confronting our truths. Because this is a process and because there are often layers of injury to uncover, I again encourage you to do this work with an experienced health care professional or trusted recovering expert, program, or group. If you feel safe and strong in moving forward without the assistance of a professional, pace yourself. Move slowly and pause when necessary. Your work at this stage is three-fold:

    a. Conducting a fearless inventory around areas of vulnerability, of weakness, or of injury. Identifying physical, emotional, psychological, and environmental triggers; naming and targeting involvement in unhealthy behaviors, destructive relationships, or toxic influences; and/or tenderly uncovering deeply embedded injustices.

    b. Acknowledging and addressing their impact upon your being and how they have contributed to or sustained periods of relapse or regression.

    c. Working through a healing process or program to recover from these injuries, influences, or injustices and to reclaim your real self. Tremendous healing can be achieved in individual therapy; however, there is also immeasurable growth and recovering available in support groups /programs.

2. As you continue working through any underlying issues, reclaiming your truths, and you are experiencing new levels of relief and renewal, it is important to commit to making your wellness a priority. What changes need to be implemented in order to create and sustain a healthy supportive environment? What boundaries need to be in place and with whom? What protective measure or controls need to be instituted? What support systems need to be revisited or invited into your way of being? Are there other measures that need attention?

3. How has your own ego—or an over-reliance on self—been a barrier to
    your recovering in the past? What can you do differently this time that
    will help to diminish that from re-occurring?

4. What new truths can you claim? What lessons can you take with you in
    moving forward?

Eight—Sheets of Rain

Spring 2011

Springtime in the Central Valley can be quite warm, but the sunshine is a welcome relief from the brisk windy days of winter. The early mornings provide opportunities for solitary walks save for the sounds of pop-up sprinklers and noisy rain-birds shooting water across the thirsty lawns. One unusually warm morning as I strode quickly down my usual path of travel, I noticed how the grass glistened when the sun cast its rays at just the right angles. Silky flower peddles that moments earlier were drooping with heaviness perked up and curtseyed, displaying their full beauty. The new arrival of leaves on barren branches created miniature waterfalls as tiny pockets of water filled their cupped formations, overflowed, and then spilled onto fragile but thirsty infant buds. Studying their resurgence reminded me how important it is to remain open to the process of renewal. Even with the hard work of breaking through the restraints of relapse or regression and of reclaiming avenues of wellness, it is essential to provide oneself with a continual source of cleansing and refreshment. Although there were times where I personally struggled with the concept of forgiveness, I knew that releasing oneself as well as others from blame was imperative to a continual recovering process. As I slowed my pace just slightly, I noticed a long canopy of green that laced itself through arched trellises leading to an open green belt. Moving through the space and feeling the mist-makers gently spraying the dry ivy while cooling my skin, I thought of the power of water and of its healing gifts.

*   *   *

There is nothing in Nature that shares such loud but subtle messages as the quiet summer storms that come up from the Gulf of Mexico and make their way into Southern California. They tend to sneak upon us with wispy cirrus clouds floating in and quickly transforming into dark bulky cumulous cotton balls. As they meander through the skies like shadows longing for their owners, white zippers flash in the distance and dance a sort of jig. Within seconds, a thunderous tympani roll simultaneously pounds the heavens and shakes the earth, announcing the arrival of rain. A few drops start to pelt the tops of trees as well as roofs; then without pause, shimmering sheets of rain begin streaming down from invisible hooks high above. The crystal clear lines of water fall in unison demonstrating their strength and force. As the sheets descend upon mountain species and man-made structures, octaves of splashing sounds reverberate through Nature's hallways. Just when the senses are able to take in the magnificence of it all, the water pins break away from heaven's lines and the wavering sheets of rain fall to the ground and disappear into the thirsty soil. With luck and with Nature's fickleness, many more surprise surges from the Gulf will grace us with their gifts before the season is over. They are ours for the taking; it is up to us to acknowledge them, open them, and if we so choose, utilize them for our wellbeing.

The gift of cleansing is the most noticeable after the first of the summer showers. The once tired and weary pine trees appear refreshed and their posture substantially erect. Near their base lay broken branches and cracked cones snapped from their weakened tethering and millions of weathered pine needles blanket the forest floor. Top heavy poplars and fully developed oaks seem relieved and lightened by the removal of unnecessary weight as dead dry leaves are tossed into the air and whisked away down the nearby rushing creeks.

Overgrown lazy grasses and thick brush are simultaneously sheared and thinned by the force of the falling waters leaving them naturally pruned and poised for renewal. Throughout the forest, evidence of the old and of the ugly is gone.

After Nature's giant washing passes through, another astounding gift that greets us is the sight and smell of the clean air. The baby blue hues in the sky are streaked with the sun's rays creating a chandelier of clarity. And the crisp fresh aromas emanating from mossy green ground create a potpourri of calm and of peace. Visibility extends far beyond the horizon and the stillness within allows Nature's lens to focus on paths before her. And as She has promised, Mother Nature clears the way for seeds of hope to germinate and take hold.

* * *

As I continued to walk under the shaded archway, I thought about how I, too, welcomed the opportunity to clean out the old and the ugly. Although there are many venues which lend themselves to an internal washing, writing was the tool which came naturally and comfortably to me. Listening to the thunderous pulse within and waiting for the lightening to signal its urgency, I began to journal sheets and sheets of words as the storms of release moved in. When the pressure mounted and the bulky clouds opened up, the rains of residual anger, sadness, and resentment streamed out of my fingers and onto my paper. With each torrent came the washing away of all the remaining carcasses of grief, shame, and blame. And as the wall of words flowed from my soul to the tips of my fingers, I felt the remnants of the past dissipate and disappear; I felt forgiveness take their place. As each successive storm moved in and then out, the releases came more quickly and more easily as there was less and less brokenness to wash away. By the end of the summer storms, my body stood strong and erect; my mind was lightened and refreshed; and my spirit was poised for renewal.

And just as nature promised, as the cleansing subsided I was overwhelmed by the resurgence of my healing truths and thus the re-emergence of my healthy being. The internal and external forces which grounded me re-surfaced and awaited my embrace, and a long-forgotten foreign emotion entered my soul—a streak of hope. It was with this refreshing ray that I could sense the aromas of calm and peace seep into the now cleansed and vacant fissures within. Just as the forest that so desperately welcomed the rains and slowly absorbed the nourishment deep within its soil, I too, allowed the infusion of renewal to enter gently, and a little at a time, relishing every ounce of vision and of purpose. As the weeks passed, I began to navigate from a previously familiar position of strength and confidence. To my surprise, my voice returned in full force, sometimes startling me with its volume of truth and with its intensity. The messages coming to me could not be silenced nor could they be ignored.

Slowing my pace, I ran my fingers through the soft silky ivy that clung firmly to the arched trellises which supported its growth. I marveled at the fragility of each leaf and at the strength of the woven mass surrounding me. Reaching the end of the shaded lush womb, I paused before stepping out into the beaming light before me. The newly found stillness within me was forming a solid platform from which to navigate; and yet, my truths maintained a poignant voice and fought for their rightful presence. Before stepping out into the heat of the sun, I glanced back at the rows of mist-makers suddenly playing in unison; I closed my eyes and listened. Hearing the splashing sounds of the spraying mist against the mural of ivy, my mind went back to the mountain storms, envisioning the sheets of rain and their relevance to the renewal process. I reminded myself that with the washing away of the old comes a window open to the new. It is window filled with possibilities and promise; at the same time, honoring one's truth requires strength and courage. I opened my eyes, turned around, and peered out across the green belt. Far off in the horizon, there was a faint outline of a solitary mountain. It tugged at my spirit and I remained focused on it; it was up to me to claim the truths before me. Returning to my betrayal environment was not a mistake; it offered me the opportunity to root out internal invaders and to remove their legacy. Regressing into an old self afforded me the humility from which to release the past and the grace from which to begin again.

I stepped out from underneath the canopy and was greeted by Father Sun. Feeling insignificant under His every-reaching rays of warmth, I was grateful for this powerful lesson. Our humanity is sometimes our most formidable opponent when it comes to fully embracing our healing journeys. Letting go of our pain and trusting our Source, in whatever form is meaningful to us, is our greatest strength. It is necessary in order to move forward.

Returning to my brisk walk and feeling energized by the trust within me, I no longer felt the need to run away—from anyone or anything. However, it was time for a change; it was simply time to move forward. I longed for the mountains and for the environment which complimented my way of being so completely. Focusing on the lonely mountain silhouette, I recalled the rambling range by our house that sculpted the horizon with its peaks and dips. I remembered how my senses became intoxicated by the crystal-clear crisp air that permeated the skies and lingered through the forest. For the first time in several years, I felt my lungs expand as I inhaled my truths and breathed life into them. Mountain Air awaited my return.

Chapter 8—Topics for Journaling & Recovery Work

1. An essential part of the healing process in any form of recovering is finding a venue to release and/or forgive oneself as well as other individuals, places, and things. Write about your venue or the ways that are meaningful and purposeful for you in letting go of the painful past. Also, describe the feelings and emotions that are important for you to release and why. Talk about who or what you need to forgive and why. As you do this, honor your voice and reclaim your being.

2. As we have discussed in several chapters, many times it is our humanity or reliance on self that remains a stumbling block in the process of releasing or forgiving, and thus, arrests our relapse. However, it is in "our humility to release the past that we receive the grace to begin again." Journal about your Higher Power, your Source, your God, your Faith, or your Belief System that speaks to you and moves you into a place of meaningful submission or of a humble acceptance. Write about the transformations you feel as you move through this process.

3. When we utilize the process of releasing and forgiving, we receive an array of "gifts". I talked about the gifts of cleansing my spirit and of clarifying my perceptions. What gifts have you experienced or are you experiencing as you continue to clean out the old and make room for the new?

The Fourth Wind—Facing South

"To the south, from where warmth comes, and rest,
and growth and color and life..."

—Kent Nerburn

Nine—After the Mountain Fire

Summer 2011

It wasn't long after moving back to the desert lands of Southern California that I was reminded of the reason why it is not for everyone. The unforgiving heat of the summer was lingering way past its seasonal tenure. Its intensity kept visitors delaying their return and motivated its residents to venture out to cooler grounds. Although I welcomed the warmth, there were days when I longed for the reprieve that the mountain peaks surrounding me provided. One sweltering Sunday afternoon, after packing up my computer and other necessary writing materials, I headed up the familiar mountain highway of years past. After climbing the steep grade for about fifteen minutes, I eagerly turned off the air conditioning and greeted the fresh breezes entering through open windows. At 1200 feet above sea level, the drop in temperature was remarkable. I continued to higher ground.

Within a half hour, I reached an elevation of approximately 4000 feet. Anxious to take in the full refreshment, I pulled into one of the vista points nestled periodically along the narrow highway. Parking off to the side and safely near the edge of the mountain cliff, I climbed out of my truck and walked over to the methodically spaced boulders, which served both as protective barriers and as scenic benches. Finding one that suited my need to view the vast high desert terrain was an easy task. I perched myself comfortably on the broad surface of a square-shaped grayish stone and breathed in the clear, clean cool air. Far below and barely within the eye's reach, I could see scatterings of the desert cities that lined the valley.

Although I felt my body relax in the quiet freshness of the altitude, I was grateful for the desert and for its nurturing provision in my life. Living here for the past several months reminded me that after we have integrated healthy supportive tools and healing strategies into our recovering journeys, we must ready ourselves to embrace whatever changes are necessary to move beyond any levels of complacency or to prevent internal contagion from unhealthy external triggers. Although routine and familiarity do provide security and confidence, welcoming new patterns of behavior or inviting healthy environments into our ways of being are essential for continual recovering from relapse or regression. Making decisions to separate ourselves from toxic relationships, or to sever ties completely with destructive forces and influences, or to stand up against anyone or anything that does not support or enhance our recovering are essential steps for continual growth. Shedding the old is indeed hard work and is often met with strong resistance, not just from our past ways of thinking but also from others who selfishly do not want their ways of life disturbed. However, it is through this process of choosing supportive healing change that we reclaim our self-respect and we posture ourselves for limitless regrowth and renewal.

Glancing toward the southern direction of the landscape, I thought how amazing it was that in a relatively short distance, the plant life changed drastically from the desert flora. With the higher elevation came increased precipitation and thus the potential for hearty sprawling vegetation. Walking back to my vehicle, I thought about how even a minor change in our recovering path can bring a new level of healing. I chuckled to myself as I thought about how we sometimes fight things that are so simple or are right in front of us. If we are just willing to take the chance and to step out of our comfort zone just a bit, there is fertile ground all around us.

Driving further up the mountain, I approached the same acreage that was destroyed by massive wild fire many years previously. Although there was not a vista point on which to park, I pulled into a small turnout that was adjacent to one of the most damaged areas. After nearly twenty years, there was almost no evidence of its devastation. Peering through a thicket of pine and sagebrush, I could barely make out a lone, charred branch angled awkwardly between the lush gardens towering above it, and I was amazed by the foliage that filled in the forgotten burial grounds of the previous forest. The unmarked gravestones of the burned remnants were replaced by thriving wild oaks and adolescent pines struggling for growth and independence. Wild brush, cacti, and sage gathered around the bases of larger plant life like children hugging onto their guardians and longing for attention. Long grasses with bountiful bouquets of purple and yellow flowers nudged their way through the crowded forest hallways and decorated the mountain floor with their sights and their smells. A curtain of leaves and needles waved across the tops of trees as winds gently lifted them up to the sky and then allowed them to descend in a graceful dance. At first sight, the forest's beauty was both overwhelming and breathtaking. With a second glance, the magnificence of it all seemed implausible given the degree of devastation and the ensuing negligence of its caretakers since the fire.

Humbled by Her beauty and resilience, I thought about how Nature found Her way back. As I studied Her fullness, I was reminded that it was a process with fluid ebbs and tides; and yet, there was a steady stream of purpose that guided the journey. Overcome with gratitude and humility, I returned to the lessons She taught me along the way. I leaned back in my seat, closed my eyes, and allowed Nature's cool breeze to take me though the past six months and to guide me through Her masterful teachings.

*   *   *

First, Nature remained still. Once the fire overtook Her, She acknowledged its power over Her. She understood its force and its potential for future danger. In remaining quiet, Nature positioned Herself in a posture of awareness and of awakening. And She remained patient. Through patience, She was able to be present and to be one with Her true self. Learning from and embracing these two insights, I purposely made an important decision. After leaving my betrayal environment, I returned to far-away soil that was familiar and safe. Many years previously, the hot and often humid desert sands were actually my first refuge from my betrayal environment. For a couple of years, I found solace in the sprawling silence and serenity of the vast beige landscape that was so splendidly outlined by the chocolate mountains surrounding it. The warmth of the desert penetrated my being and I remembered how it triggered the beginning of the first thaw of my frozen spirit. Returning first to the desert seemed a natural transition as I continued to nurture myself and protect my growing truths. Spending days resting in the quiet of the summer desert calmed me and began to center me. There was no rushing this process as the pieces that had fallen away needed time to flow back into my being, attaching where they fit, or making room for future growth. I had to work hard at being still. I reminded myself that being still allowed me to reframe the three previous years and to utilize their reference as a tool for future navigation. Hours and hours of solitude made room for peace to weave its way through every fabric of my soul. I allowed very little outside human influence into my place of stillness. Frequently, the sounds of soft Native American recorder music accompanied my recital of reflection, and I felt an infusion of tranquility enter my lungs.

With each day and week that passed, an appreciation for the promises of staying in the present took hold, and I felt myself start to reclaim my way of being.

Secondly, Nature trusted in the process. No one came to rescue Her or rebuild Her after the fire. Nature knew that She would have what She needed in order to begin again; She knew her blanket of ashes contained the exact nutrients the soil required in order to produce growth. And She moved slowly. Nature understood that the process could not be rushed; doing so would sabotage its legitimacy and its longevity. I, too, trusted in the healing process. A veteran of it, I realized that time was not my enemy, but my friend. Giving myself the gift of time alone allowed my ashes to cultivate in a compost of serenity and authenticity. Treating myself to solitary months of self-care and self-comfort blended in with other healing ingredients provided fertile grounds from which to plant my new-found spirit. It was also important at times to just be—to let things settle and solidify. Nature taught me that sometimes the most significant change comes so slowly that it is barely visible. And, what is going on underneath or within the process is often more valuable than the evidence of it. Thus, there were many days where I spent time in reflection, or prayer, or in writing where I listened to my inner being. As I did so, my truths continued to formulate and ferment. They continued to enrich my soul.

Thirdly, Nature grew one step at a time. The dormant roots of species buried beneath the rubble slowly emerged from their imposed hibernation and provided the source for regrowth. One of the first perceivable signs of life after the mountain fire were small patches of soft lush green moss growing on the burnt twigs and branches nestled closely to the soil. As the fall and winter months brought additional precipitation to the grounds, the spring rolled out a massive carpet of lime-colored flooring. The following summer, fragile sprouts of grasses and flowers popped up out of the black and green checkered soil. Within the next year or two, small sage brush plants and a few tiny cacti poked their bodies through the budding grounds. With each new birth, Nature waited while its integration formed. She made space for its development and allowed time for its growth to take hold. Most importantly, She tested its levels of independence and dependence upon Her.

Nature provided protection where needed; She granted autonomy where it was earned. And so it was with me as well. As I started to reclaim my truths and experience their development within me, I kept a pulse on their levels of strength and of consistency. I tested my grounds of navigation to foreign and familiar places, and I noted feelings of resiliency or lack of them. With each success or setback, I readjusted my boundaries, expectations, and degrees of exposure. Most importantly, I took ownership of my choices, and thus, carefully and thoughtfully made decisions based on healthy progress. Each day and each week, I felt stronger and stronger; however, I kept in mind that strength does not necessarily equate to endurance. It is always important to remember the length of the race and who or what is in it. Thus, I set realistic goals with reasonable expectations. By healing a little at a time, I realized that it not only builds character, but it also nurtures confidence. I reminded myself that the majestic pine trees took the longest to return, and that their magnificence was not diminished because of it. In fact, it was indeed their gradual but steady re-emergence that truly empowered them and sustained them. As I continued to recover a day at a time, I treasured each new sprout of truth that popped through my fertile soil. More importantly, I felt my recovering take hold as more mature growth filled in the barren inner landscape and breathed life into my being.

And finally, recalling the splendor of the towering thriving foliage, Nature reminded me of Her most subtle but powerful lesson—wellness speaks for itself. The plant life was plentiful, and the animal life had rediscovered their favorite nesting and feeding grounds. However, Nature's recovery was best evidenced by the healing beauty which emanated from within and which permeated the environs with quiet confidence and completeness. As I continued to find my way back to the wellness I longed for, I too found that my voice took on a posture of calm and quiet. Where there were once smoldering ashes filled with narratives recounting the past, as well complaints as to where I needed to be, my story now was one of purposeful authenticity evidenced by my well way of being. As nature exemplified so well, when recovering is solidly integrated into the foundations of fertile soil, there is no need to boast of its existence. As the stillness within me grew and spread, I felt myself become fully alive—breathing in my truths and letting them speak for themselves.

*   *   *

Opening my eyes, I allowed myself time to soak in all of Nature's teachings. However, with the splendor of fullness and completeness before me, Nature displayed Her most masterful point. Each singular lesson of Nature proved invaluable to the process of recovering, and yet all of Nature's lessons combined encompassed an over-riding theme. In losing Herself, Nature held true to who She was; and in doing so, She found her way back. Deep down inside, each of us knows what our truths are. It is forgivable to lose them; it is unforgivable not to reclaim them. Although it takes an incredible degree of courage, of commitment, and of self-compassion, returning to living a life of authenticity is the driving force behind finding our way back. There is no greater lesson; there is no greater gift to ourselves.

As I continued to reclaim my truths, I was able to see the path ahead more clearly. The beauty and tranquility of the desert provided me with the respite I needed, but I was ready for change and eager to continue my journey. I had one more mountain to find!

Chapter 9—Topics for Journaling & Recovery Work

1. After we have come through a period of relapse or regression, it is important to take inventory of the lessons learned and to integrate them into our ongoing recovering process. In Chapter 9, I disclosed the lessons that not only sustained me throughout my journey but that also proved to be invaluable insights as I moved forward. Journal about any or all of the following four topics or other lessons that have become an essential part of your journey. Spend as much time on this as needed. Be thoughtful and introspective. What you have learned from your past, what new levels of awareness you have embraced, and what new truths you have adopted that will serve you well as you achieve new levels of healing?

   Lessons to journal about:

   a. How have you *remained still and patient*? How have you allowed for the development of an awareness to truth and an awakening of self to take hold?

   b. How have you *trusted in the recovering process*? In what ways have you given yourself the gift of time in order to cultivate healthy ways of being?

   c. How have you demonstrated that you are *healing one step at a time*? Describe how you are keeping a pulse on current levels of strength and consistency; testing environments of navigation and reassessing levels of healthiness; recognizing set-backs and making adjustments; and taking ownership for choices.

   d. How are you *allowing wellness to speak for itself*? Describe what it feels like to be at peace with your way of being.

2. Relapse is about losing who we are and forfeiting our potential for what we are meant to be. As I stated at the close of this chapter, "Deep down inside, each of us knows what our truths are. It is forgivable to lose them; it is unforgivable not to reclaim them." What are your truths? How have you already claimed them and how will you continue to do so? What additional decisions, changes, or sacrifices have you made or will you continue to make in order to support their integration into your authentic self. How will you continue to be true to yourself?

Ten—Mountain Air

Present

Leaving the sprawling bleached desert in search of higher ground,
Traveling southeast across miles of sand and sage.
Scattered remnants of western towns showered in blowing dust,
With dilapidated RV parks strangely positioned among broken signs of life.

Between the battered towns of Hope and Salome tired cyclists peddling against the wind,
Wondering where they came from, where they are going—and why.
Over two hours of flatlands followed by endless acres of cotton fields,
With no workers in sight and machinery left standing—questions remain.

Into the third hour, a turn northeast begins the ascent,
Thicker greener brush fills in the gaps between boulders and barbwire fences.
Mysterious ranches are hidden at the ends of roadways that disappear into the hills,
And a big small town with the name of Congress uncannily appears in the middle of nowhere.

Heading north, the once straight highway becomes a maze of twists and turns,
Climbing higher and higher, a teasing by a few pines creates an appetite for more.
Slowing down, the grade steepens as the dense foliage provides barriers from the cliffs below,
Around every corner, anticipating the smells and the sights—not much longer.

Reaching the top of the last plateau—magnificence in waiting,
A valley filled with monstrous pines, wild oaks, and a potpourri of Nature's beauty.
A slight descent brings into view the first signs of a bustling historic town,
And a row of picturesque B and B's nestled among the trees invites new-comers into its arms.

Settling into a cozy room and then setting out to explore,
Discovering a park with a wooden gazebo adjacent to a massive stone Court House.
Extraordinary memories surface of childhood summers spent in a safe far-away place,
Children playing, friendly faces walking their dogs, and visitors resting in the shade.

A day of meandering through the shops while local artists display their crafts,
Native American influences make their presence known with subtle and gracious strength.
A rowdy saloon sits juxtaposed by an elegant Bistro with white tablecloths,
The old meshing with the new—the indigenous embracing recent transplants.

Returning to the Inn with a full stomach and a peaceful heart,
A feeling of home starts to emerge—the blend of Nature with humans.
A lonesome coyote announces the end of another day,
And the smells of nightfall fill my lungs—cool, crisp, and clean.

Awakened early by a chorus of cicadas and by the excitement of it all,
A cup of coffee warms me as I sit in the private courtyard, soaking in the calm.
Giant pines soar upwards, creating a clear lens to the sky,
I close my eyes and take in a deep breath of Mountain Air.

I am home.

Epilogue

As I sit at my computer, I look out my office window and see a new but familiar sight. A few feet from me are majestic pines, sprawling oaks, and lanky grasses sprouting from underneath smooth rocks and broken boulders. The air is cold. Small patches of snow remain on the ground from a winter storm of weeks past. Often times, I catch a glimpse of deer sauntering up and around our back deck foraging for their early meal. On a few occasions, I've watched a small herd of Javelinas roam our property, and I find myself both disgusted and amused by their grotesqueness. Once again, our home is perched on a hill; not as high or as isolated as our first home in the mountains, but every bit a mountain dwelling. Once again, I am breathing mountain air.

One of the many rewards of recovering from relapse is the process of discovery. Once we open our minds and our hearts to possibility of change, newness awaits us. Not only do we view life differently, but we experience it differently. We are not simply going through the motions, but we are embracing and celebrating each day and what it offers us. Although I never thought of leaving California or the beloved mountain area where we once lived, after researching and exploring a similar community in a neighboring state, we have discovered another beautiful place to live. Although I readily embrace the healing lessons of the past, I am open and excited to learn from the present and to invite renewal on a daily basis. New lessons are available and abundant; they are ours for the choosing.

Another reward of recovering is the uncovering of ourselves. Once we are out from underneath the blanket of shame that has weighed us down, we are free to become and to be our true selves. By living our lives in authentic and purposeful ways, we reinstate our worth, dignity, and respect. As we continue to heal and as we continue down our paths to wellness, we are called to reach out to others in need of support and guidance. We are to use our journeys to help others who are hurting. Although I am an author of clinical works, writing this book and disclosing my personal journey was not what I set out to do. However, if I am to live out what I believe and trust in what I teach, I too must do so with honesty and integrity. In uncovering my truth, honoring its impact in my life, and in sharing it with you, I am free.

Lastly, one of the finest rewards of recovering is basking in its ease. During an episode of relapse or in a period of regression into unhealthy behaviors, thoughts, or feelings, life is hard. It is painstakingly complicated; it is excruciatingly destructive and debilitating. Whether one is struggling with addiction, staying in a toxic relationship, returning to a place or person who does not respect the rightful position and posture of your being, or whether you have dishonored your own expectations, boundaries and ways of being, relapse guarantees one thing—suffocation of the self. As I shared my own experience, I openly disclosed the slow progression of losing myself. I often used the phrase, "I could not breathe", or, "As the days passed, I found it harder and harder to breathe." However, as we work our recovering processes or programs and we begin to heal, our thoughts clear; our minds open up; and our truths flow. We navigate comfortably as we live congruently with who we are and who we are meant to be. Life is meaningful and purposeful. The self is at ease; it is free.

For each of us, finding the way back to wellness means we will take many different paths. And yet, we will all share a similar journey. We will each find our own truths and we will breathe life into them.

As you are climbing your recovering mountain, remember—*take it one breath at a time.*

Remember—rejoice as you reclaim yourself in the process.

About the Author

In Her Own Words

Typically, I am an author of clinical works writing to bring healing and hope to others. Of course, there is always a piece of me and of my experiences in them as well. When I sat down and started writing *Mountain Air*, I did so solely for my own recovering. Writing is a significant tool that I utilize in my healing process. It wasn't until after I finished the very rough and rambling first draft that I felt it may be of benefit to others. Even then, I wasn't sure. It took many more rewrites, time away from the drafts, and the integration of a stronger, more powerful voice into my being which ultimately fueled my desire to share my narrative with you.

Mountain Air, as you have read, is a unique perspective into the topic of relapse and recovering from it. As you know now, I based this work on my own debilitating decline into emotional relapse. I shared with you how returning to my betrayal environment of my youth precipitated the relapse, and I described how the myriad of triggers within those surroundings exacerbated my struggle. I also disclosed the unearthing of a deeply embedded injury from my childhood—a sexual assault—which was at the core of my descent into relapse. Throughout the writing of *Mountain Air*, it was always my intention to make this book about the emotional and psychological challenges that accompany any kind of relapse—shame, self-blame, guilt—after sustaining a period of wellness, of sobriety, or of integrity to one's way of being. At the same time, I am guessing that there are many readers who are wondering why I did not fully disclose the details of the abuse I endured. I want to explain why. There are two explanations; both are extremely important to me.

First, it is my belief that individuals, even those who share common abuse experiences, heal differently and uniquely. For many, it is extremely helpful and healing to share their experiences in a very public forum and to include the details of their injuries or injustices. Indeed, there are many celebrities as well as non-celebrities who have shared their most private and painful stories on television as well as through other media venues. Their narratives reach out and help many people; they educate and inform others; and hopefully, most importantly, the survivors themselves experience additional healing each time they reveal their histories. For me, and many others like myself, this is not the case. My healing came in the trusting of two therapists and in the process that it took to peel off the layers of injury—a little at a time and over a lengthy period of time. In the safe harbor of experienced, nurturing therapists, I was able to disclose all the intimacies of my pain. However, in the retelling of the abuse, I do relive it and thus, I re-traumatize myself. I also feel as though I give my power over to the betrayers and that I diminish my "voice" in doing so.

Therefore, I must value my healing truth. I choose to keep my experiences contained because in doing so, I am respecting myself and my choices, and I am honoring my betrayal experiences with the dignity and grace that serve me well.

Secondly, and as importantly, I do not want to be remembered as a survivor of abuse who endured a litany of injustices. I want my legacy to be one of renewal and of refinement. In my last book, *Breaking Through Betrayal: And Recovering The Peace Within,* I talk about the difference of being "defined by our betrayal experience" or of being "refined by it". It is paramount that my recovering message to you be one of "moving beyond being defined by our survival identity and embracing the opportunity to become a more effective being and to be more elegant in the process". I want others to remember how I taught them to seek ways to enhance and cultivate new ways of being, and that I encouraged and motivated them to act upon those choices. It is vital that when others think of my writing and my works that they will find and embrace the excitement in polishing, perfecting, and honing their continued journeys, and that they will cease to be encumbered by the labeling as a post-abuse being. From my book, *Breaking Through Betrayal,* I challenged you to release your self-label and to capture your refinement—who you are now and what you have become:

> "I want you to think of yourself as a gem—a diamond. You dug yourself out of the deepest recesses of a dark mine; you allowed yourself to be chiseled, and chipped; you chose the process of being precisely crafted and uniquely shaped into a new form. You have prepared yourself for the final touch—the polishing. As you gently cultivate and hone the intimacies and intricacies of your being, your elegance will surface. As the polishing process proceeds, feel the purity, the true value, and the authenticity of the precious stone, of you, come through."

If I am to honor my refinement, I must live it out—not just for myself but also as an example to you. If I am going to leave the legacy that I hope to, I must safeguard the integrity of my healing tenets, and I must hold steadfast to my truths. As your healing journey unfolds, I encourage you to do the same.

With wellness and warmth,
Holli

Breaking Ground (Aug. 1990)

Alexis grows up amongst the pines

Home (Garner Valley, CA)

Dan enjoying free time

Mom and Alexis (2011)

Home (2011 – Prescott, AZ)

Bibliography

_____(1985). *Al-anon's twelve steps & twelve traditions*. New York: Al-Anon Family Group Headquarters, Inc.

Beattie, M. (1987). *Codependent no more: How to stop controlling others and start caring for yourself*. Center City, MN: Hazelden.

Beattie, M. (1989). *Beyond codependency: And getting better all the time*. New York: Harper & Row.

Beattie, M. (2009). *The New Codependency; Help and guidance for today's generation*. New York: Simon & Shuster Paperbacks.

Gilbert, E. (2006). *Eat, pray, love: One woman's search for everything across Italy, india, and indonesia*. New York: Penguin Books.

Kenley, H. (2010). *Breaking through betrayal: And recovering the peace within*. Ann Arbor, MI: Loving Healing Press.

Lawrence-Lightfoot, S. (2009). *The third chapter: Passion, risk, and adventure in the 25 years after 50*. New York: Farrar, Straus, and Giroux.

Markova, D. (2000). *I will not die an unlived life: Reclaiming purpose and passion*. Berkeley, CA: Conari Press.

Morrow Lindbergh, A. (2003). *Gift from the sea*. New York: Pantheon Books.

Nerburn, K. (2002). *Neither wolf nor dog: On forgotten roads with an indian elder*. Novato, CA: New World Library.

Nerburn, K. (2009). *The wolf at twilight: An indian elder's journey through a land of ghosts and shadows*. Novato, CA: New World Library.

...And a Source of Inspiration...

I would like to acknowledge author Kent Nerburn whose writings—*Neither Wolf Nor Dog* and the *Wolf at Twilight* inspire me.

Thank you for their imagery, wisdom, and spirit.

Index

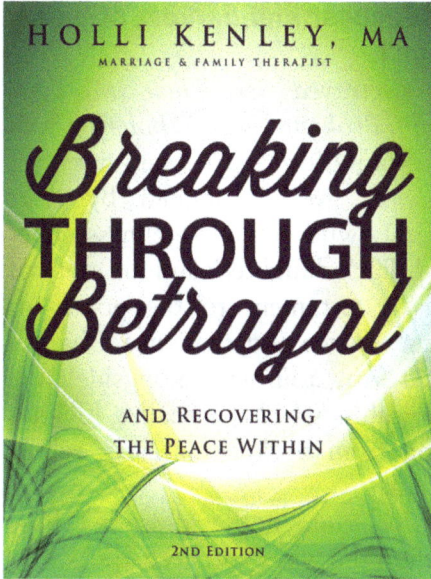

Are you ready to heal?

Breaking Through Betrayal: And Recovering the Peace Within is for any individual who has experienced betrayal and is struggling to break through its bonds. Through a proven process tailored for recovery from betrayal injury, readers are invited to:

- Explore and connect with the different kinds of betrayal: rejection or abandonment; a violation of trust; a shattered truth or belief.

- Identify and move through betrayal's three States of Being – confusion, worthlessness, and powerlessness - while uncovering contributors of symptom intensity and duration.

- Revive and restore mind, body, and spirit with a 5-part recovering process for "righting oneself" and attend to re-occurrence or re-injury.

New in this Second Edition of *Breaking Through Betrayal*, readers are offered a unique perspective on a timeless topic -- *relapse*. By reframing relapse as a familiar experience and redefining it as an issue of self-betrayal, readers are:

- Drawn into a safe conversation while breaking through the stigma, secrecy, and shame of returning to any kind of unhealthy pattern of thinking, behaving, or feeling.
- Invited to partake in an empowering 6-part recovering process in moving from self-betrayal to self-discovery.

"Useful for anyone caught in self-blame, shame or repeated victimization...this empowering 'in-control' approach can help readers take charge, assess injury, gauge healing and find excellent strategies to protect themselves from future trauma when relating to one's betrayer."
—Beth Hedva, Ph.D. author of award-winning *Betrayal, Trust and Forgiveness*

"Holli Kenley shares her comprehensive approach to a situation most of us experience at least once in our lifetimes – betrayal. She takes a complex topic and turn it into an uncomplicated and well-organized read, including easy-to-follow exercises at the end of each chapter. An important resource for anyone experiencing grief and loss as the result of betrayal."
—Janet A. Hopkins, Editor-in-Chief, *In Recovery Magazine*

The daughters' stories touch upon the deepest and darkest of pains: knowing you have a mother... but you don't.

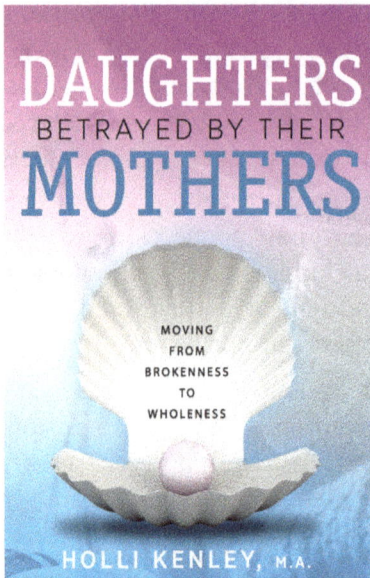

Daughters Betrayed By Their Mothers: Moving From Brokenness To Wholeness is an intimate exploration into the lives of daughters who were wounded by their mothers and who chose wellness over victimhood. Each daughter's unique story of recovery is a testament to the power of choice, perseverance and resilience. Readers are invited to journey alongside the daughters, grabbing hold of healing lifelines and moving from broken places to whole spaces within.

Do you feel your mother did not "show up" for you in the ways you needed?

- Because of your mother's role in your life, do you feel like you were "not enough?"
- Do you wonder if it is possible to heal from the brokenness that comes from being wounded by your mother?

If you answered "yes" to any of these questions, the "Daughters" warmly welcome you.

"There are tears of both sorrow and joy in the beautiful, brave stories of harm and hope. Daughters Betrayed By Their Mothers changed my life."
—Charlotte Carson, Editorial Director, ClearLifeMagazine.com

"*Daughters Betrayed By Their Mothers* is heartrending and uplifting; dark and optimistic; painful and inspirational. A profound human document."
—Sam Vaknin, author of Malignant Self-Love: Narcissism Revisited

"Powerful, reflective, and reassuring to all who read it, Holli Kenley's *Daughters Betrayed By Their Mothers* reminds us that no matter what hurt we have experienced, the opportunity to heal and be whole is always possible."
—Cyrus Webb, media personality, author, and speaker

"So much of what Holli illustrates through her research is that one of the most important relationships —the mother/daughter bond—can be the key to understanding relationship patterns throughout life."
—Kiersten Hathcock, founder Little Light Project, Inc., a non-profit organization

Learn more at www.HolliKenley.com
From Loving Healing Press www.LHPress.com

Look for Holli Kenley audiobooks on Audible.com and iTunes

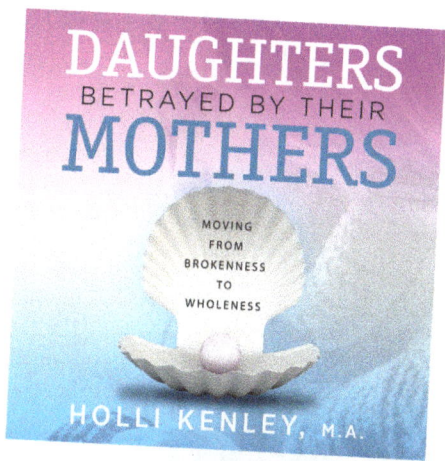

DAUGHTERS
BETRAYED BY THEIR
MOTHERS

MOVING
FROM
BROKENNESS
TO
WHOLENESS

HOLLI KENLEY, M.A.

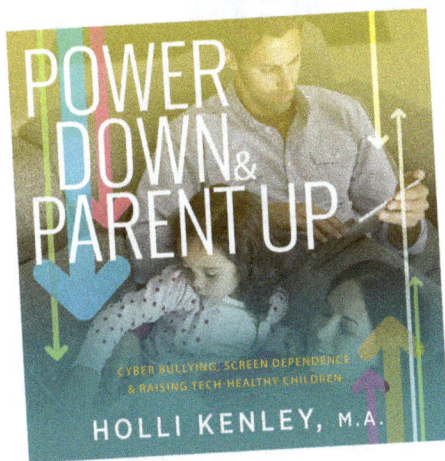

POWER
DOWN &
PARENT UP

CYBER BULLYING, SCREEN DEPENDENCE
& RAISING TECH-HEALTHY CHILDREN

HOLLI KENLEY, M.A.

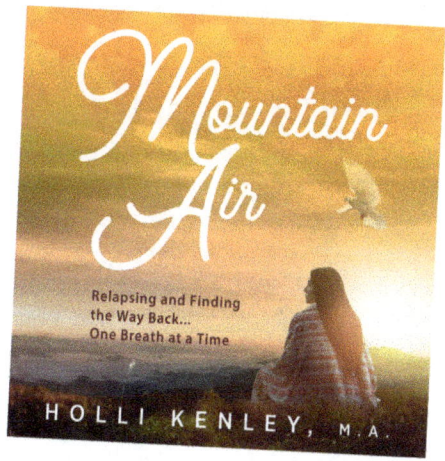

Mountain
Air

Relapsing and Finding
the Way Back...
One Breath at a Time

HOLLI KENLEY, M.A.